EUCALYPTS

Volume I

EUCALYPTS

Volume I

STAN KELLY

Text by G. M. Chippendale and R. D. Johnston

NELSON

Thomas Nelson Australia Pty Limited
19-39 Jeffcott Street West Melbourne Australia

First published 1969
Reprinted 1974, 1976
Reprinted 1977 as *Eucalypts, Volume 1*
Reprinted 1978, 1979

ISBN 0 17 001861 X

Printed in Hong Kong by
South China Printing Co Ltd

Contents

Plates

Preface to the Plates

More than twenty-five years ago a friend of mine suggested that I should paint the Australian eucalypts which we admired so much. In those days colour photography did not reproduce the definition needed for anyone other than a trained botanist to identify specimens. I still feel that watercolour is the best medium available for clear colour reproduction, and I think it has the boldness necessary for this unique flora. Soon afterwards I began painting eucalypts exclusively and it became my ambition to paint every variety.

Through my work as an engine driver with the Victorian Railways, and through contacts made travelling in the Northern Territory, the Kimberleys, elsewhere in Western Australia, and Queensland I have gathered my specimens, but I feel these traditional supplies have now been exhausted, and I will have to rely on state Forestry Commissions, Herbariums and my own travels to complete the collection. The paintings have been exhibited, but I would never sell any of them, and once I have completed a variety I never paint it again.

Apart from its botanical significance, the object of this book is to arouse a wider general interest and appreciation of a genus which is truly Australian. If it prevents the destruction, or inspires the planting of a single tree, then its purpose will have been fulfilled.

I should like to thank the many friends and enthusiasts who have assisted in collecting specimens, especially the late Fred Couzens, who, through the Waite Agricultural Research Institute, was an unfailing source of supply, to A. Hargreaves and E. Muir, whose interest inspired my work, to A. Lindner, G. Althofer, R. Fields, R. Middleton, R. Higginson, R. Phillips, Miss H. M. Lang, G. Hateley, Miss H. Hateley and finally G. M. Chippendale and Dr R. D. Johnston for their invaluable assistance in identifying specimens and writing the text.   STAN KELLY

Ararat
March 1969

Authors' Preface to the Text

Many aspects of the genus *Eucalyptus* are currently being studied by various workers in the fields of taxonomy, chemotaxonomy, ecology, anatomy and forestry. The results of this work will eventually be published in scientific papers and will affect presently accepted concepts of the relationships among species and the arrangement of the species in a system of classification.

The only systematic arrangement available at present in published form and covering the whole genus is that of W. F. Blakely in *A Key to the Eucalypts* (third edition, 1965). Although it is recognised that some species are misplaced in Blakely's arrangement, it is still used as a standard reference, and the order in his book has been followed in the present publication.

Identification of *Eucalyptus* specimens still presents a major problem. Various keys to assist in identification have been devised, but none is completely satisfactory. There are keys for limited geographical regions, but these may be misleading if the species in question is not included. The usual form of such keys presents the user with a series of 'either ... or' choices, so that complete material is necessary; lack of buds, fruits or juvenile leaves may make a decision impossible. Because of the unsatisfactory operation of such a dichotomous key, and the complexity needed if one were to try to cover the variations in all species, no key has been included in this book.

Because there are some species not in this book, and because it is impossible to reflect the range of variation of a species in one illustration, we advise caution in the identification of eucalypts. Most species can be clearly identified by reference to Stan Kelly's excellent plates, but if there is doubt, and if a critical identification is needed, the services of the appropriate Government Botanist should be called upon. A specimen bearing leaves, buds and fruits, with accompanying notes on location, size, and bark type, is suitable for this purpose.

A number of the plates show the twigs in a pendulous position, and while many eucalypts have this character, there are a few of those illustrated which we would have preferred to see in an erect position as being natural for the particular species. However, we have accepted that Mr Kelly has arranged these for artistic effect.

We hope that our exhaustive index will help readers to find particular groups of species.

There is a vast amount of information available on eucalypts, and we offer the following collection of references on the subject. Some will give formal botanical descriptions which we have not attempted, considering the coloured plates accompanying our text.

Anderson, R. H. *The Trees of New South Wales*, fourth ed., Government Printer, Sydney, 1968.

Beadle, N. C. W., Evans, O. D. and Carolin, R. C., *Handbook of the Vascular Plants of the Sydney District and Blue Mountains*, published by the authors, Armidale, 1962.

Black, J, M., *Flora of South Australia*, Part 3, second ed., Government Printer, Adelaide, 1952.

Blackall, W. E., revised by Grieve, B. J., *How to Know Western Australian Wildflowers*, Part 1, University of Western Australia Press, 1954.

Blake, S. T., 'Studies on Northern Australian Species of Eucalyptus', *Australian Journal of Botany*, Vol. 1, No. 2, 1953, pp. 185–352.

Blakely, W. F., *A Key to the Eucalypts*, third ed., Forestry and Timber Bureau, Canberra, 1965.

Burgess, Colin, *Blue Mountain Gums*. Wildlife Preservation Society of Australia, Sydney, 1963.

Carr, S. G. M. and Carr, D. J. 'Convergence and Progression in Eucalyptus and Symphyomyrtus', *Nature* 196, 1962, pp. 969–72.

Chippendale, G. M. (editor), *Eucalyptus Buds and Fruits*, Forestry and Timber Bureau, Canberra, 1968.

Costermans, L. F., *Trees of Victoria*, published by the author, Melbourne, 1967.

Curtis, Winifred M., *The Student's Flora of Tasmania*, Part 1, Government Printer, Tasmania, 1956.

Eichler, Hj., *Supplement to J. M. Black's Flora of South Australia*, Government Printer, Adelaide, 1965.

Gardner, C. A., 'Trees of Western Australia', *Journal of Agriculture of Western Australia*, Vols. 1–7, third series and fourth series, 1952–66.

Hall, N. and Johnston, R. D., *Forest Trees of Australia*, Forestry and Timber Bureau, Canberra, 1962.

—— *A Card Key for the Identification of Eucalypts*, Forestry and Timber Bureau, Canberra, 1964.

Hall, N., Johnston, R. D. and Marryatt, Rosemary, *The Natural Occurrence of the Eucalypts*, Leaflet 65, Forestry and Timber Bureau, Canberra, 1963.

Johnson, L. A. S., *Studies in the Taxonomy of Eucalyptus. Contributions from the New South Wales National Herbarium*, Vol. 3, No. 3, 1962, pp. 103–26.

Johnston, R. D. and Marryatt, Rosemary, *Taxonomy and Nomenclature of Eucalypts.* Leaflet 92, Forestry and Timber Bureau, Canberra, 1965.

Kelly, Stan, *Forty Australian Eucalypts in Colour*, Dymocks, Sydney, 1949.

Maiden, J. H., *A Critical Revision of the Genus Eucalyptus*, Government Printer, Sydney, 1903–33.

Penfold, A. R. and Willis, J. L., *The Eucalypts*, World Crops Series, Leonard Hill, London, 1961.

Pryor, L. D., 'Species Distribution and Association in Eucalyptus', *Biogeography and Ecology in Australia*, edited by A. Keast, R. L. Crocker and C. S. Christian, Uitgeverij Dr. W. Junk, The Hague, 1959.

There are many other references, particularly in scientific literature, on this interesting subject.

In the matter of names of eucalypts, we have endeavoured to use the name which is correct according to the International Rules of Botanical Nomenclature. Also, in species which have two or more varieties, these Rules result in the specific name being repeated for the typical variety. For example, *Eucalyptus leucoxylon* var. *leucoxylon* refers only to the typical form of this eucalypt, and does not include the other varieties which are referred to by their own names, *E. leucoxylon* var. *macrocarpa* and *E. leucoxylon* var. *pauperita*. Where a species has no described varieties, it is not necessary to repeat the specific name, so that, for example, *E. polyanthemos* includes all forms regarded as this species.

Canberra
February 1969

G. CHIPPENDALE
R. D. JOHNSTON

To My Wife

—STAN KELLY

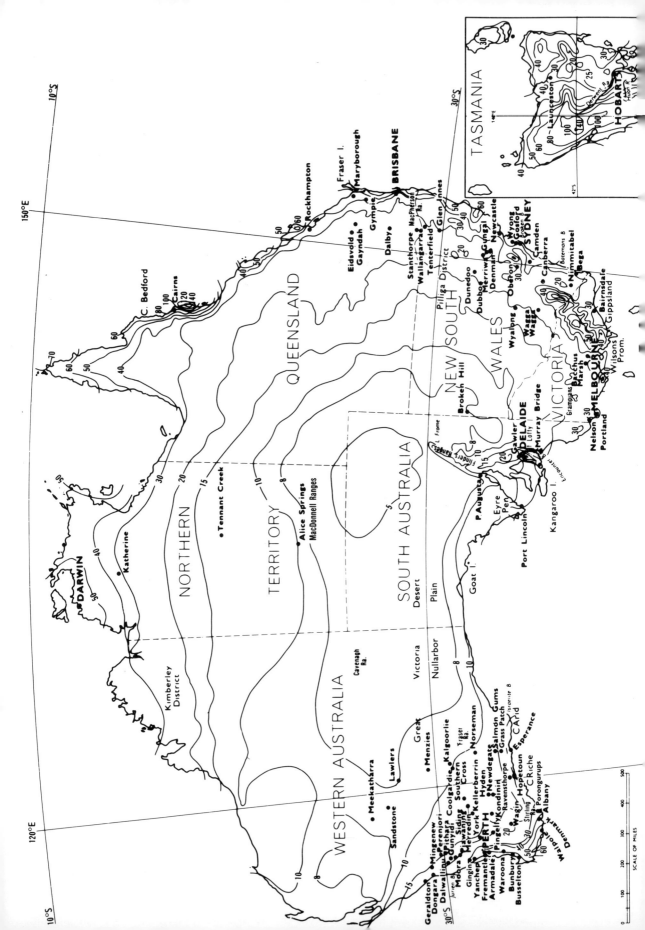

Introduction

EUCALYPTS are the most conspicuous element of the Australian vegetation, for they constitute about ninety-five per cent of our forest trees and dominate the woodlands. In fact, the typical Australian scene is one in which eucalypts appear, for they are found from east to west and from north to south of the land.

Although most species occur naturally only in Australia, there are a few which extend to the islands to the north. New Guinea and Timor have representatives, and one, New Guinea gum (*Eucalyptus deglupta*), extends to the Celebes and the Philippines. This is the limit of natural occurrence, however. None occurs in New Zealand, nor in the western part of the Indonesian archipelago; and in spite of the ubiquitous appearance of red gums in the Mediterranean region, or blue gums in California, these trees are the result of introductions from Australia.

Ranging from the semi-arid sand plains and dry watercourses of central Australia to the tree-line of the Snowy Mountains, the eucalypts have, with considerable success, evolved to survive Australia's conditions. The only genus which rivals them in numbers or consistency of representation in the vegetation is *Acacia* and, although the acacias, or wattles, are more numerous in the drier regions and have some species which occur in the rain-forests beyond the limits of eucalypt occurrence, few can rival the size of the eucalypts and where they occur together the acacias generally form an understorey. The eucalypts, too, may be reduced in size under the harsh conditions towards the limits of their range. At the tree-line, over 6,000 feet above sea level, we find twisted, wind-swept shrubs and on the shallow soils of the sandstone plateaux in the eastern tablelands, many-stemmed whipstick mallees may grow to less than three feet high. But as conditions ease, as the soil becomes deeper or a valley provides some shelter, the shrubs become small trees and these in turn give way to taller trees until, on the deep, loamy soils of sheltered valleys the trees become the tallest hardwoods in the world, with columnar trunks lifting the leafy crowns over 300 feet from the earth. Similarly, the whipstick mallees, whose stems barely reach an inch in diameter, contrast with the huge tallow-wood trees, whose buttressed trunks may be twenty feet in diameter.

Even amongst trees of the same size, there are conspicuous differences in form and general appearance, some having long, bare limbs, with tufts of fine, feathery leaves at the ends, whilst others have short, stubby branches and dense, round crowns. Some have long, willowy branches, others are stiff and upright; each, in its native environment presents a characteristic form which enables it to be recognised at a distance.

Each species also has its own range of conditions where it occurs naturally, although these conditions are not always those in which it grows best. Often a less vigorous or less shade-tolerant species cannot compete on the better sites but, because it is able to tolerate harsher conditions, can grow on shallow soils, or is frost-resistant, it survives where the more vigorous cannot. Thus there is a pattern of distribution of species which is related both to competition and to the environment. On the one hand the local climate, influenced by the regional climate and by the local topography, operates through maximum and minimum temperatures, seasonal supply and demand of water, and the effects of wind. On the other hand, the soil, which is influenced by the local rock type, topography and climate, determines what nutrients are available to the tree, how the water supply is regulated, and the physical support of the tree against gravity and wind. By a process of natural selection over many generations, species have developed to grow in each of the many combinations of conditions.

Often the ranges of tolerance for environmental conditions and the competitive abilities of several species are similar, and these species occur together, to form an association. Eucalypts are normally outbreeding, however—cross-pollination of flowers on separate trees is easier than of flowers on the same tree—so that, unless there is some restricting influence, the various species in an association will hybridise, to produce a swarm of intermediate forms. There is a limited amount of hybridisation, in fact, although occasionally one finds an apparent merging of otherwise distinct species; in general, associations of different species are able to maintain their identities because there are barriers to their interbreeding.

The number of species and varieties of eucalypts which are recognised by different botanists varies, but it is generally accepted that there are about 450 more or less distinct forms, plus many hybrids both natural and artificial.

The characters which are used to distinguish these species include the form of the plant, its bark, foliage, flowers, fruit and seeds. All these characters should be taken into consideration, but some features have been found by experience to be much more reliable, in that they show consistent differences between species, and these differences do not vary greatly with changes in growing conditions.

Form, or habit of growth, often shows considerable variation within single species. For example the red bloodwood (*E. gummifera*) of coastal New South Wales may occur on shallow sandy soils as a mallee, but on better sites will grow to 120 feet tall. Many species do have characteristic form, however. The rose gum (*E. grandis*) of New South

Wales and Queensland is typically tall and straight with a long bole free of branches, whilst calgaroo (*E. parramattensis*) usually has a short, crooked trunk and spreading crown. Differences in form are also related to the ability to form lignotubers—swollen masses of woody tissue at the base of the stem—which forms a reservoir of dormant buds at ground level. Those species which consistently have well-developed ligno-tubers are able to sprout quickly following such catastrophes as bushfires, and the strong development of this tendency results in the mallee habit, where the plant has a large, woody root-stock and several stems of approximately equal size. Mallees occur typically on 'difficult' sites, where shallow soils, frequent fires, or other restrictions to growth give an advantage to those plants which are able to regenerate quickly, but on better sites they are usually overtopped by species which produce a single, tall stem.

There are several distinct types of bark which are characteristic of groups of closely related trees. The bloodwoods, for example, usually have rough, short-fibred, persistent bark on the trunk and large branches, and this bark becomes cracked in an irregular pattern of roughly rectangular, and more or less scaly, pieces. The height to which the rough bark extends from the base of the trunk varies considerably between species, and the spotted gums (*E. maculata* and *E. citriodora*) have completely smooth stems which are usually beautifully mottled in blue, grey, pink and white.

The ironbarks, as the name implies, are a group of species which characteristically have hard, dark, deeply furrowed bark. Again, there are species with smooth limbs, and yellow gum (*E. leucoxylon* var. *leucoxylon*), otherwise a member of this group, normally has a smooth, yellowish bark. Within the group there is some variation in bark structure, the broad-leaved red ironbark (*E. fibrosa* ssp. *fibrosa*) has a flaky and rather soft bark, whilst on the grey ironbark (*E. paniculata*) it is corky.

There is another group with persistent bark extending to the small branches, called stringybarks, because of the strongly fibrous bark which is usually brown and often coarsely furrowed. The true stringybarks are a closely related group, but rather similar bark is found on several trees which do not resemble stringybarks in other characters. They are usually distinguished by other names, for example the mahoganies, but Darwin stringybark (*E. tetrodonta*) and Bailey's stringybark (*E. baileyana*) are names used because of a resemblance in this single feature for these species which do not resemble stringy-barks in any other way.

Rather less fibrous than the stringybarks are the peppermint barks. Their group name comes from the characteristic odour of the oils in the leaves of several species in this group. Typical peppermint bark is fibrous but closely and finely interlaced, usually grey on the surface but brown within. Again the extent of the persistent bark over trunk and branches varies amongst the different species, being reduced to a short 'stock-ing' in the river peppermint (*E. elata*) or being totally absent from the white pepper-mint (*E. linearis*).

Typically, species of the box group also have closely adhering, finely fibrous, grey bark over all or part of the trunk and branches. This bark is similar to that of the pepper-mints, but boxes do not have the characteristic oils of the peppermints, and can be distinguished in other ways. The boxes are fairly closely related to the ironbarks, and hybrids between these groups are common. As would be expected, the hybrids have bark which is intermediate between the parental types, more fibrous than ironbark but harder than box bark.

The ash group of species usually have rough, more or less fibrous bark on the trunk, but smooth bark on the branches, the amount of rough bark being characteristic of each species, so that, for example, white ash (*E. fraxinoides*) usually has a very short stocking, whilst messmate stringybark (*E. obliqua*) has fibrous persistent bark extending to the small branches. The texture of the persistent bark and the colour of it and of the smooth bark help to distinguish the various species.

Each of these groups consists of closely related species, with many other features in common, but the commonest bark type is the 'gum', in which the whole trunk, or all but a short part of the base, is smooth. These trees are not all closely related; gums occur in almost all the recognised groups of eucalypts and in fact most young trees have smooth bark. The gums shed their bark in various patterns. Many lose the whole of the outer layer each year, usually in mid summer, and these species have the smoothest, cleanest appearance. Many are covered in a white, powdery bloom, which enhances their attractiveness, and these are the species which are most popular as specimen trees. Probably the best-known example is the ghost gum (*E. papuana*) of central Australia but others such as rose gum (*E. grandis*) can be just as brilliantly white.

Other gums shed their bark in patches of various shapes over periods of two or more years. The bark surface changes colour as it weathers so that an attractive mosaic results. The red gums and the grey gums have this type of bark. Often the newly exposed surface is bright yellow, older areas are silvery grey, whilst the oldest are dark grey or brown. Some species, such as brittlegum (*E. mannifera* ssp. *maculosa*), combine the powdery surface with a patchwork of soft, pastel shades, which brighten where the trunk is polished by rubbing branchlets, and glow red in summer just before the bark is shed.

The scribbly gums are aided in their development of a distinctive bark type by insects which spend part of their life cycle beneath the outer layer of bark, eating their way along a double line of convolutions. When the bark is shed the insect has departed, but its signature is left as a scribble on the smooth surface. Although only a few species are known as scribbly gums, this feature is common to a large number of related species. It can be seen, for instance, on the smooth upper bark of the ashes or on the snow gum (*E. pauciflora*) and provides a useful way of separating species which grow together and otherwise look very similar.

The pattern of development of eucalypt leaves is very interesting. All seedlings produce their earliest leaves in pairs, opposite one another on the stem. This arrange-ment is thought to represent the ancestral form, for related genera in the same family such as *Angophora*, always have opposite leaves. In the adult form, however, most eucalypts have their leaves arranged alternately on the stem, or two successively to the left, then two to the right. Between the seedling and the adult most species have one or more intermediate forms of leaves. These are frequently opposite, or almost so, broader than the adult form, and in many cases covered by a waxy bloom, so that they appear silver, bluish, or grey-green. The duration of this intermediate form, and the ease with which the plant reverts to it, vary considerably amongst the groups and some species, such as the Argyle apple (*E. cinerea*), rarely produce adult leaves in natural conditions, although they often do so when grown in gardens. The white-leaved mallee (*E. albida*), a Western Australian species, often has creamy white juvenile leaves on some branches of mature trees.

Another feature which changes between the juvenile or intermediate leaves and the adults is the attitude of the leaves. Most juvenile leaves are held horizontally and have distinct upper and lower sides, whilst the adults are mostly pendant and there is little difference between the two surfaces. The young trees, therefore, and regrowth after injury on older trees, may look quite different from the adults. At the same time it has been found that some species which in the adult form are extremely difficult to separate, have quite different juvenile leaves. Probably the best examples of this are mountain gum (*E. dalrympleana* subspecies *dalrympleana*) and manna gum (*E. viminalis*). In the former, the juvenile leaves are ovate and glaucous, whilst in the latter they are narrowly oblong and green.

The leaves, like the bark, show distinctive features which are associated with the different groups. For example, the bloodwoods have adult leaves which show marked differences between the upper and lower surfaces and have fine regular veins which run across the leaf at a wide angle to the midrib. Other groups, the Sydney blue gums, red mahoganies and grey gums also have leaves which are darker on the upper surface and have widely diverging venation, whilst the red gums have leaves which are the same colour on both surfaces and rather less regular venation. In contrast, some of the mallees, such as *E. formanii*, have very fine, narrow leaves with no secondary veins visible. Between these extremes we find that the ashes typically have sickle-shaped leaves, the same colour on both surfaces, with conspicuous veins at an acute angle to the midrib, whilst the snow gums have almost parallel venation.

Eucalypts have oil glands in the leaves and produce several different types of oil, various combinations being characteristic of particular species, or even of local populations within the species. Minor industries have developed in various parts of Australia based on the distillation of these oils for commercial purposes.

Very few species produce their flowers singly; the most well-known are the Tasmanian blue gum (*E. globulus*) and the mottlecah (*E. macrocarpa*) of Western Australia. More usually, the flowers are borne in inflorescences which may be simple and produced in the axils of the upper leaves, or compound and produced at the ends of the branchlets. A few, such as Gympie messmate (*E. cloeziana*) and brittle gum (*E. michaeliana*), have compound inflorescences in the leaf axils.

The bloodwoods, having large flowers borne in many-flowered inflorescences at the ends of the branchlets, are often very showy and the red-flowering gum (*E. ficifolia*), with its masses of bright red flowers, is one of the most popular flowering native trees in Australia. Other colours, ranging from cream to deep pink, are commonly found on cultivated trees which are probably hybrids of *E. ficifolia* and the closely related marri (*E. calophylla*).

Many other species produce coloured flowers, but because they are carried within the crown of the tree they are generally less showy. Even so, the masses of colour which show through the foliage of coral gum (*E. torquata*) or Strickland's gum (*E. stricklandii*), or the colourful buds and contrasting flowers of illyarrie (*E. erythrocorys*), are worthy of comparison with any flowering tree.

Eucalypt flowers do not have sepals and petals; a few species have small teeth which represent the sepals, but in the vast majority the calyx and corolla form two super-imposed caps, the outer of which is shed early in the development of the flower whilst the inner is shed as the flower blooms. One large section of the genus has a single cap, or operculum, formed by the early fusion of both calyx and corolla.

The shape and sculpture of the operculum is one of the features used to identify species. Another feature, which is the basis of the present system of classification within the genus, is the shape of the anthers and the way they open to shed their pollen. Anther shapes vary from more or less oblong, with parallel slits, to kidney-shaped with diverging slits, and box-like opening by pores. There are many minor variants but the major types correspond to the major groups based on consideration of many characters.

Probably the most useful single item for identifying eucalypts is the fruit. Eucalypt fruits are capsules, that is, they are dry, many-seeded vessels which shed their seeds at maturity. They range in size from as small as a match head to more than two inches across, and may be fragile and papery or hard and woody, stalked or sessile, and with a wide variety of shapes. The outer covering of the body of the fruit, which was the calyx-tube of the flower, usually shows a circular scar where the operculum was attached. Inside this is a second scar, the staminal ring, and within this again a ring of tissue, known as the disc, surrounds the openings of the capsule. The relative widths of these rings, and whether the top of the capsule is enclosed within the fruit or protrudes in the form of teeth, are characteristic of each species, and, taken with the size and shape of the fruit, are often sufficient to enable the species to be identified.

Again, groups of species have similar fruits. The bloodwoods have more or less ovoid fruits, many with the opening contracted to form a neck. The disc lines the neck and the teeth or valves are enclosed within the fruits. In contrast, the red gums have globular fruits with a broad, raised disc and projecting, often woody, valves. Many of the stringybarks have raised hemispheric fruits with a flat disc and small valves.

The classification of eucalypts is based on consideration of all these features. Many species are similar in some respects but distinct in others and it is not always easy to identify species without collating a lot of information about them. This had led to confusion in the past and in some cases we have several names which all apply to the same species. Even today there is need for further work to show what variations occur within single populations of species and what the relationships are between various populations.

The fact that there are many variations within species has been used to some advantage by horticulturists, but there is considerable scope for further work in this field. Colour variants are common amongst the Western Australian species, red, pink, yellow, or cream forms occurring in otherwise similar plants. Coloured flowers are much less common in eastern Australian species but even here trees with red or pink flowers have been seen in normally cream-flowered species, and single pink flowers are fairly frequent, although these may be associated with abnormal flowering.

Similarly, dwarf forms of a few species are already in cultivation and it is known that seedlings of apparently 'good' species show considerable variation in size and vigour. Careful selection may produce forms valuable for horticulture.

A second method of producing different forms which may be useful in cultivation is by hybridisation. Apart from the many individual trees of supposed hybrid origin which can be found in natural populations, hybrids between related species which do not grow together have been produced by artificial pollination, or have been found in seed from planted trees, and some of these are worthy of cultivation.

Unfortunately, seeds from the hybrid trees produce very variable progeny, so that in order to produce more trees of a particularly desirable hybrid it is necessary either to go back to the original parents and do more controlled pollination, or to produce plants by vegatative propagation. Eucalypts do not strike readily from cuttings taken from mature trees, so that the production of cultivars is a much more difficult and expensive business in this genus than it is in many others. Nevertheless, the advantages of being able to reproduce the more attractive hybrid forms are sufficient to encourage experimentation along these lines.

The common names of eucalypts are many, and it is a minority of species which have a stable and widely used popular name. Many names are taken from aboriginal names, and a number are artificial, such as Comet Vale mallee, which is simply a translation of the botanical name *E. comitae–vallis*. A few eucalypts have no common name.

The botanical, or scientific, names have also had some instability in certain species, but the International Rules of Botanical Nomenclature are aimed at stability. In many cases, the botanical name is easier to remember and, when one knows the derivation, more descriptive or reminiscent of the particular eucalypt.

Eucalypts gave inspiration to the early Australian poets such as Adam Lindsay Gordon who wrote:

'When the gnarl'd, knotted trunks eucalyptian,
Seem carved, like weird columns Egyptian',

Will Ogilvie praised:

'Hurrah for the red-gums standing
So high on the range above!'

A. B. Paterson mentioned:

'A scent of eucalyptus trees in honey-laden bloom'.

With seemingly countless individual eucalypt trees in Australia, it may seem strange to urge their protection against destruction, but many species are being gradually eliminated. In wheat lands and farm lands, most eucalypts are restricted to small tracts, often only the land between a road and a fence. Cities grow only at the expense of tree removal. Overseas countries cultivate eucalypts for ornament, shade, and soil protection, as well as for pulp-making. So, may Australians appreciate these wonderful trees more and help in their protection.

Not all of the species of *Eucalyptus* are shown in this book, but the paintings are an excellent representative selection.

PLATE 1

ILLYARRIE (*Eucalyptus erythrocorys*)

Of all the eucalypts, illyarrie has one of the largest, and certainly the most striking and unusual budcaps. It is brilliant scarlet, square, with a raised cross on it, greatly resembling a biretta, the square cap worn by some clerics. When this unique operculum is shed, mainly from March to May, bright yellow anthers, set as a cross, form the flowers. This colourful combination of features identifies the species beyond all doubt, but the fruit is also remarkable with its central fleshy disc and undulate margin.

The budcap is referred to by the name *erythrocorys* which means 'red helmet'. Illyarrie is an aboriginal name.

Not very common, illyarrie occurs in a small area of Western Australia, south of Dongara near Bookara Siding—where it is called Bookara gum—with other small occurrences westward towards Jurien Bay. It favours sandy, or calcareous soils, and in nature forms a small tree, sometimes rather straggly, with a white, smooth bark.

Young trees of illyarrie grow straight and erect, although older trees have somewhat oblique trunks and tend to sprawl; it can grow to twenty-five feet high. It is cultivated widely in Western Australia, grows well at Adelaide, and is adaptable to most soil types, where the rainfall is at least eighteen inches annually.

PLATE 2

TALLERACK (*Eucalyptus tetragona*)

A feature of the sandy, low scrub within thirty to forty miles of the southern coast of Western Australia, and also occurring north of Perth in the area near Jurien Bay, this mallee is distinguished by its square stems and glaucous or mealy white leaves. Its hemispherical buds exhibit the feature which is recorded by the botanical name *tetragona*, referring to the four angles on the bud and consequently on the fruit capsule. As in several other related species, tallerack has its anthers in four bundles, as shown in the flowers.

Sometimes known as the white-leaved marlock, this mallee occurs only in sandy soil, growing as an open shrub. In some places near the southern coast it forms small thickets, but eastward from Esperance it is scattered in heathlands.

When cultivated, tallerack is much as in nature, growing robustly with a single stem at first but

eventually spreading. It flowers from November to January, is moderately drought-resistant, and frost-tender when young.

PLATE 3

MALLALIE (*Eucalyptus eudesmioides*)

A mallee which grows from six to ten feet high, mostly in sandy soils north of Perth, Western Australia. It forms a bushy shrub which flowers very freely between January and May. Again, as in related species *E. erythrocorys* and *E. tetragona*, the stamens are arranged in four bundles in the flower. This is regarded as a primitive feature within the development of the *Eucalyptus* genus. Additionally, small, opposite, green leaves and the buds in groups of three are characteristics which help to distinguish the species.

The bark is usually smooth brown with older bark shedding in strips low on the stems. The branches are plentiful, straight from the base.

Some older botanical literature confused this mallee species with a much taller tree species, *E. gongylocarpa*, which has been called marble gum or desert gum. However, the two species are quite distinct. The name mallalie is an aboriginal name recorded from the Murchison area.

Although rarely cultivated, this species may be effective where dense shrubs are required, particularly in exposed, sandy, coastal places, or in hot, dry areas.

PLATE 4

SANDPLAIN MALLEE (*Eucalyptus ebbanoensis*)

Mostly seen as a mallee up to fifteen feet tall, but sometimes growing as a small tree as high as thirty feet, this species is another of the group which includes *E. erythrocorys*, *E. tetragona* and *E. eudesmioides*. Again, the stamens are found in four distinct bundles when the flowers open.

The buds are always in groups of three, as in the related species, but the leaves are alternate in the sandplain mallee. The shiny, dark, red-brown capsules are an attractive feature.

Originally found between Mingenew and Dongara in Western Australia, the sandplain mallee has now been recorded eastward to north of Kalgoorlie; it grows mainly in sand or sandy loam in low, mixed, eucalypt scrub.

The species is drought-resistant and moderately frost-resistant, and as a mallee it would be an excellent hedge or windbreak. However, the few cultivated specimens seen have been small trees, with red twigs.

PLATE 5

DARWIN STRINGYBARK (*Eucalyptus tetrodonta*)

This is sometimes called messmate in northern Queensland and in the Kimberley area of Western Australia. Associated with Darwin woollybutt, (*Eucalyptus miniata*) in a tall, open forest community in these areas and in the area between Darwin and Katherine in the Northern Territory, this tree is a dominating feature of the vegetation. Enjoying a monsoonal rain as high as sixty inches annually, the Darwin stringybark grows straight to about sixty feet, and sometimes forms a pure stand within the forest in the drier, sandy sites. It has rough, grey, fibrous bark on the trunk and branches.

The species is distinguished by having its buds in groups of three, the rim of the calyx tube being markedly undulate, and its stamens are in a continuous ring like those of its close tropical relative, the Sturt Creek mallee (*Eucalyptus odontocarpa*).

Ludwig Leichhardt, in his account *Overland Expedition to Port Essington* referred to this eucalypt when he mentioned that the aborigines made boats 'of the inner layer of the bark of the Stringybark tree'. He also assumed that the timber would be useful for building, and although it is not a highly durable timber, it has been used locally to a limited degree.

PLATE 6

SCARLET GUM (*Eucalyptus phoenicea*)

The orange-red flowers, the narrowly urn-shaped capsule, and the narrow leaves help to distinguish this attractive species from its nearest relative the Darwin woollybutt (*E. miniata*). It grows as a slender tree up to thirty feet on stony hills in shallow soil, mainly in the northern part of the Northern Territory, but it has been found in the Kimberley area of Western Australia. Although widely spread in this region, it is not very common, often occurring as single trees. Scarlet gum has yellowish-brown, rough bark on the trunk with the branches smooth and reddish.

The species name *phoenicea* is a reference to the brilliant, crimson plumage of the mythical bird Phoenix.

Most reference books apply the common name 'Ngainggar', but this was an aboriginal name applied

to a plant in Queensland at Cape Bedford, far from the known range of the scarlet gum, and therefore this name is not applicable.

Seed of this gum has been sought for tropical planting, as it grows in a hot climate with monsoonal rainfall. It could become a valuable cultivated species.

Flowering begins about January and continues until May.

PLATE 7

DARWIN WOOLLYBUTT (*Eucalyptus miniata*)

Woollybutt is associated with the Darwin stringybark (*E. tetrodonta*) in a tall, open forest covering large areas of northern Queensland, northern parts of the Northern Territory, and of the Kimberley area of Western Australia. In these areas it occurs in tropical sands, and particularly dominates the wetter sites of the forest and in sandstone hills.

Features of the Darwin woollybutt are the profuse, brilliant orange flowers from June to August, and the dark reddish, rough, brittle, woolly-like bark which covers most of the trunk, with the branches smooth and white. It is related to scarlet gum (*E. phoenicea*).

The name *miniata* is from the Latin meaning 'coloured with red lead', referring to the flowers. Some references give this species the common name 'melaleuca gum', which was originated by Ludwig Leichhardt, but this name is neither in use nor suitable in areas where the tree grows.

Being accustomed in nature to a monsoonal rainfall of sixty inches in a hot region, *E. miniata* should be a spectacular specimen in coastal, tropical planting. It will flower at about four years old when about four to six feet high.

Although producing trunks of about twenty feet, which is half the total tree height, the woollybutt is not a good timber species as it is subject to termite attack and often hollow in the centre.

PLATE 8

SQUARE-FRUITED MALLEE (*Eucalyptus tetraptera*)

This species is cultivated in other parts of the world as well as within Australia. In nature it is an untidy, straggling shrub, attaining only about four feet in height and growing in poor, sandy soil often near sandstone outcrops. It is only found between Israelite Bay and the Stirling Range in Western Australia.

The name *tetraptera* means four-winged, and this refers to the large, square fruit with four marked angles or wings; this is a unique feature, and the red-capped bud is also outstandingly different from all other buds. The leaves are extremely thick.

Its unusual characteristics make this mallee an interesting novelty plant. In cultivation it can become straggly, as in nature, but careful pruning can make it somewhat bushier. Sometimes in cultivation it becomes a small tree with smooth, grey bark, and it flowers from April to July. This mallee is moderately drought- and frost-resistant.

PLATE 9

STEEDMAN'S GUM (*Eucalyptus steedmanii*)

First collected by Henry Steedman in 1928 and several times subsequently, this eucalypt has only been collected by two other people, C. A. Gardner and L. J. Teakle. The area has been given, rather vaguely, as Forrestania or in the vicinity of this former agricultural settlement which failed and was soon deserted. This was east of Hyden and south of Southern Cross in Western Australia, but the species has not been collected or refound by anybody since 1938.

Steedman's gum is a dense, rounded tree growing to about thirty feet high, with attractive, smooth, red-brown bark and an occasional strip of older bark adhering. The four-angled buds and the exserted valves of the fruits help to separate the species from the fuchsia gum (*E. forrestiana*). Flowers occur in midsummer.

Fast-growing and suitable as an ornamental, a lawn species or a windbreak, Steedman's gum is moderately drought- and frost-resistant. In the past, some nurseries have sold other eucalypts as this species. Usually in these cases, the species concerned was *E. spathulata* var. *grandiflora*, but fortunately the genuine species is also in cultivation.

PLATE 10

ROSEBUD GUM (*Eucalyptus erythrandra*)

Originally this was described as a true species of *Eucalyptus* but later evidence has shown that it is a natural hybrid between *E. tetraptera* and *E. angulosa*. It occurs in small areas in sandy heath country between Esperance and Ravensthorpe in Western Australia where it grows as a mallee or shrub to about eight feet.

In cultivation it is sometimes weak and drooping, but eventually attains eight feet or so, with smooth, grey branches and trunk. It flowers irregularly, and apparently briefly, between March and October.

The rosebud gum is an attractive species, but its close relative, the square-fruited mallee (*E. tetraptera*), would be preferable as a garden subject, as it grows in similar situations, has a similar appearance, but flowers more regularly.

PLATE 11

CARBEEN (*Eucalyptus tessellaris*)

Carbeen varies from a stunted tree about forty feet tall to a moderately large tree, but it is distinctive no matter what the size, for it has a short stocking of persistent bark which changes abruptly to a smooth, light grey surface. The persistent bark is dark grey and cracked into small rectangular segments like tiles, and it is to this feature the name *tessellaris* refers.

The crown of carbeen consists of slender white branches with drooping twigs bearing long, narrow, dull green leaves. These usually have fine, regular veins at about forty-five degrees to the midrib.

This species is found over most of the eastern half of Queensland and extends a short distance into New South Wales. It is normally found on level or undulating country, with a wide range in soil texture, but grows best on deep, sandy loams. The area where it occurs has a summer rainfall, the annual amount varying between fifteen and sixty inches, and only in the southern part of the range do frosts occur.

Carbeen is an attractive tree, flowering in summer, and because it is resistant to heat and drought, is suitable for ornamental planting in tropical areas.

PLATE 12

GHOST GUM (*Eucalyptus papuana*)

W. F. Blakely in his book *A Key to the Eucalypts* (1934) mentions 'drooping white gum' as the common name for this species. The name 'carbeen' has also been used, although this name is applied to other species too. It is comparatively recently that the name 'ghost gum' has been used, and this is certainly now widely used by people living in the areas in which it grows, and by tourists who visit these outback areas.

Several trees about thirty miles west of Alice Springs, used as models in water colour paintings by

Albert Namatjira, have become magnets for photographically-minded tourists. When insects attacked these trees, Government employees were sent to cut off infected branches!

Smooth, powdery, white trunks topped by bright green, drooping foliage are distinctive features, but some people wrongly identify grey-trunked river red gums (*E. camaldulensis*) as ghost gums. Ghost gum grows in sandy soil on rocky hillsides and on alluvial plains, attaining between forty and fifty feet in height. It is found in northern and western Queensland, the Northern Territory and the Kimberley area of Western Australia as well as in Papua. It flowers rather lightly from December to February.

PLATE 13

ROUGH-LEAVED RANGE GUM (*Eucalyptus aspera*)

As well as the common name above, this species has been called brittle bloodwood. Probably neither name is used by people who live in the area in which it grows. The trees grow mainly in the twelve to thirty inch rainfall areas of the Northern Territory, and in adjacent areas of Queensland and Western Australia. It is not a common species, being scattered in occurrences which are usually on stony soil on hillsides or ranges, and it can grow from twenty to forty feet high.

Distinctive features are the smooth, white trunk, sometimes with a few feet of rough, tessellated bark at the base, and the small, rough, sessile leaves which are responsible for the specific name *aspera*, meaning 'rough'.

The rough-leaved range gum is supposed to flower about September, but it is doubtful if accurate records are available for naturally-growing plants. Similarly, although it may be a useful species for cultivation in semi-arid areas, it has not been tried and very few, if any, nurserymen have the seed or plants in stock.

PLATE 14

ROUGH-LEAVED BLOODWOOD (*Eucalyptus setosa*)

This is an inhabitant of shrublands and mixed open forests mainly in the northern part of the Northern Territory and adjacent areas of Queensland and Western Australia, where it usually grows on rocky ground. It reaches up to thirty feet in height, but is more often from twelve to twenty feet high,

sometimes being rather crooked in growth. Scattered occurrences are found in the sandy spinifex areas of central Australia near Tennant Creek, and in these parts it is known as desert bloodwood.

The bark is grey and flaky. Bristle-like hairs on the young growth, the buds, and sometimes on the fruits and mature leaves, are distinctive for the rough-leaved bloodwood. The specific name *setosa* is a reference to these setae, or stiff hairs. The tree was first described in 1843 from a specimen collected on an island in the Gulf of Carpentaria in 1802 by the English botanist Robert Brown and the Austrian artist F. L. Bauer who were on a voyage with Matthew Flinders.

It is recorded as flowering in winter months, but also sporadically in summer.

PLATE 15

FAN-LEAVED BLOODWOOD (*Eucalyptus foelscheana*)

While sometimes growing to thirty feet, this bloodwood usually is shorter. Smaller trees are often covered by rusty, scaly bark, but taller trees are smooth and white on the trunk with some of the scaly bark near the base. It occurs in low, savannah woodland and sometimes in the Darwin stringybark (*E. tetrodonta*) forests, mostly in sandy loam or alluvial soil, and it is often deciduous during the dry season of the monsoonal climate. The main area of occurrence is in the northern part of the Northern Territory and Western Australia.

The broad leaves and variable bark of the fan-leaved bloodwood resemble the round-leaved bloodwood (*E. latifolia*) but the former is distinguished by its larger buds which are about half an inch long, almost twice the length of those of *E. latifolia*.

W. F. Blakely considered that the species would be useful for tropical planting because of its large leaves, but it is not known to be cultivated anywhere. It is likely that it would not be deciduous in cultivation. Flowers are recorded from October to January.

The fan-leaved bloodwood is named after Paul Foelsche of Darwin who collected a specimen from which the species was first described by Ferdinand von Mueller.

PLATE 16

SWAMP BLOODWOOD (*Eucalyptus ptychocarpa*)

Occurring on the banks of streams and in moist places in the more northerly parts of the Northern

Territory and in the Kimberley area of Western Australia, this species is also sometimes referred to as spring bloodwood in Western Australia. So much is the species associated with streams that C. A. Gardner, former Western Australian Government Botanist, mentions that it can be used as an indicator of water at shallow depths.

The swamp bloodwood has similarities with the Darwin woollybutt (*E. miniata*), both having ribbed buds and large, woody, ribbed fruits. However, swamp bloodwood has grey, fibrous bark, which is more or less tessellated, and longer leaves. It is a spreading tree which can attain fifty feet in height, but is more usually only up to thirty-five feet. Flower colour varies from white to pink to red, and those forms with the more brilliant, red flowers would make a spectacular tree in cultivation. Flowering time is March and April.

The timber of swamp bloodwood is softer than that of any other eucalypt in the Northern Territory.

The name *ptychocarpa*, meaning 'folded or pleated fruit', is a reference to the strong ribs on the capsule.

PLATE 17

MARRI (*Eucalyptus calophylla*)

A dense, round-headed tree which can grow up to one hundred feet but mostly is much less, perhaps up to fifty feet, marri is also known as red gum. A feature of the famed Stirling Range in Western Australia is Red Gum Spring, so named because of the occurrence of this species. However, it grows through the jarrah (*E. marginata*) and karri (*E. diversicolor*) forests of Western Australia and extends northward to the Murchison River and southward to Cape Riche, mainly in the lighter, sandy soils.

The smooth leaves, glossy dark green above, paler beneath, are the feature which is indicated by the name *calophylla*, meaning 'beautiful leaf'. Together with the generous inflorescences and the large, urn-shaped fruits, the attractive leaves make the marri distinctive. The flowers in February and March are usually creamy white, but there are some naturally occurring as pale pink. The bark is rough and flaky on trunk and branches.

Marri can withstand a frost to as much as twenty-five degrees F and it is already planted in other countries, being particularly suitable to warm coastal regions with ample rain. It is good for timber, although not plentiful enough for widespread use, and

valuable for the copious nectar which is useful to apiarists.

PLATE 18

RED-FLOWERING GUM (*Eucalyptus ficifolia*)

Probably the best known eucalypt in cultivation, for many years this species was the only one thought to be a 'flowering gum' by many people. It is a rough-barked, small tree growing from thirty to forty feet in cultivation, but only to about thirty feet in its natural habitat. It is dense and round-crowned, and its scarlet flowers can cover the tree in the period from December to February. Some forms have white or pink flowers. It is restricted to small areas in the region between the towns of Denmark and Walpole, west of Albany, on the southern coast of Western Australia, where it grows in poor, sandy or gravelly soil, but it has been found to be adaptable to other soils.

The red-flowering gum occurs in an area of sixty inches annual rainfall and prefers a minimum rainfall of thirty inches, but will grow in lower rainfall areas if adequate ground water is available. It also prefers a frost-free situation, needing protection from frosts for at least the first year.

Already widely planted throughout the world, the red-flowering gum grows best in coastal areas, and it has been found to be suitable as a street tree for both shade and ornament.

The capsules of this species have often been used as 'woggles' in securing the scarf worn by Boy Scouts.

PLATE 19

BROWN BLOODWOOD (*Eucalyptus trachyphloia*)

The bloodwoods are characterised generally by rather large, compound inflorescences which are borne at the ends of the branchlets. Because the individual flowers are usually rather large, these trees are quite showy when in flower. Brown bloodwood, however, has small flowers, from January to March, followed by small fruits, and is probably the least spectacular of the group. Also, the fruits are rather fragile, whilst most of the bloodwoods have woody fruits.

This species has an unusual distribution, occurring close to the coast in south-eastern Queensland and northern New South Wales, on medium quality soils, and on shallow, rocky soils further inland, near

Eidsvold in Queensland and near Denman in New South Wales. Further inland still, in the Pilliga district, it is common.

Apart from the small fruits, brown bloodwood is identified by its yellow-brown, rather flaky bark and the narrowly oblong juvenile leaves. It may grow to over a hundred feet on good sites but is more often much smaller. It is not an outstanding tree for horticultural purposes.

The name *trachyphloia* means 'rough-bark' which, though suitable, could apply to many species.

PLATE 20

BLOODWOOD (*Eucalyptus terminalis*)

The common names for this species have been as confused as the scientific nomenclature, for this species and the long-fruited bloodwood (*E. polycarpa*) have been confused until comparatively recently. C. A. Gardner uses the name 'mountain bloodwood' for Western Australia, but this name is certainly not used in other areas where it grows, namely in the Northern Territory including central Australia, south-western Queensland, north-western New South Wales and far northern areas of South Australia.

This bloodwood forms a tree up to thirty-five feet high, and in more northerly regions it has smooth, white bark with some mottled rusty and scaly bark towards the base. In central arid areas there is more scaly or plate-like, tessellated, brown bark.

Some distinctive features are the thick leaves similarly dull grey-green on both surfaces, the usually scurfy buds, and the woody fruits which are widest below the middle. However, botanists have difficulty in identifying this species accurately without reliable, complete data. It has been given a number of scientific names because of the variation it exhibits over its geographical range, but Dr S. T. Blake, in 1953, clarified this in his *Northern Australian Species of Eucalyptus*.

The large inflorescences of creamy flowers occur from May to July. This bloodwood favours ground with good water relations, and some pastoralists have used it as an indicator when siting bores.

PLATE 21

RED BLOODWOOD (*Eucalyptus gummifera*)

E. gummifera is a typical bloodwood in having persistent, short-fibred and irregularly cracked, brown bark over the whole of the trunk and a rather dense crown of thick, glossy, dark green leaves which are paler on the underside. It has compound inflorescences of club-shaped buds, borne at the ends of the branchlets, and woody, ovoid fruits with a short but distinct neck. This short neck, the smooth, smaller branches and brown bark distinguish it from a similar species, pink bloodwood (*E. intermedia*).

Red bloodwood occurs as a tall tree up to 120 feet high, along coastal New South Wales, and extends just into Victoria and as far north as Maryborough in Queensland. Apparently unable to compete with the faster-growing species on highly fertile sites, it is most common on rather poor, sandy or gravelly loams, but it is also found on shallow sands over rock, where it may be reduced to a mallee form, with several stems only an inch or so in diameter.

Although it will grow on a wide range of soils including poor soils, this tree is confined to regions of mild climates, with rare frosts, moderate maximum temperatures and reliable rainfall. It forms a dense canopy and should be a good tree for windbreaks or shelter close to the coast, but has not been used to any extent. It flowers in late summer.

PLATE 22

YELLOW BLOODWOOD (*Eucalyptus eximia*)

Occurring only on the shallow, sandy soils of the Hawkesbury sandstone within fifty miles of Sydney, yellow bloodwood does not grow to more than fifty feet tall. It is conspicuous because of its scaly, yellow-brown bark, rather irregular crown, and coarse, curved, grey-green leaves. In late spring the large cream-coloured flowers produce a brief display, which is followed by the rather large, urn-shaped fruits. Occasionally one finds a tree which produces bright yellow flowers which have considerable promise for horticulture.

Yellow bloodwood is able to grow in soils of low fertility and rather low water-retaining capacity, in areas of more than twenty-five inches rainfall. It will stand only light frosts, being particularly frost-sensitive when young.

PLATE 23

LEMON-SCENTED GUM (*Eucalyptus citriodora*)

Lemon-scented gum occurs naturally in a relatively small region in sub-tropical Queensland, where it looks much like spotted gum (*E. maculata*), but it has been widely planted, both in Australia and overseas, and, under cultivation, is one of the most graceful and attarctive of the eucalypts.

E. *citriodora* grows to a tall, slender tree; cultivated trees have a smooth, powdery, white bark, an open crown, and fine foliage, the long narrow leaves producing a light shade which does not inhibit the growth of lower plants. Although it grows naturally on rather heavy soils in a region of moderate rainfall with a maximum in summer, it will thrive in uniform-rainfall or Mediterranean-type climates, and on deep, sandy loams as well as clays.

The characteristic scent of the leaves is derived from citronellal. This oil has been distilled for commercial purposes.

Lemon-scented gum flowers in June and July.

PLATE 24

SPOTTED GUM (*Eucalyptus maculata*)

One of the most attractive trees of coastal New South Wales and south-eastern Queensland is the spotted gum. It grows to 150 feet in height and five feet in diameter, usually with a long, straight bole and a dense crown of glossy, green leaves.

The most outstanding feature of this tree is the smooth, clean-looking bark. This is shed in irregular patches, leaving small depressions like dimples, and as the bark surface ages it changes colour, from cream to blue-grey, pink or red, giving an interesting, mottled appearance.

Spotted gum is closely related to the bloodwoods and although it has a smooth bark the inflorescence and fruits are characteristic of the bloodwood group. That is, the flowers are borne in rather large, compound inflorescences, whilst the fruits are ovoid, with a short neck and deeply enclosed valves.

Spotted gum occurs mainly on rather heavy soils, especially clay loams derived from shales, where it is often associated with grey box (*E. moluccana*) and ironbarks. It is rather large for use as an ornamental tree, but it is a valuable species for forestry, producing a hard, strong, tough timber, one of the most suitable Australian timbers for tool handles.

PLATE 25

KARRI (*Eucalyptus diversicolor*)

Karri trees can grow to 250 feet high, and thus are the tallest trees in Western Australia, as well as one of the tallest-growing species in Australia. The bark is smooth, grey to blue-grey and orange-yellow in blotches, and the leaves are distinctly paler on the under side, a feature which is indicated by the name *diversicolor* which means separate colours.

Although not as resistant to termites as jarrah (*E. marginata*), karri is one of the important timbers of Western Australia. It is hard, tough and reasonably durable, having been used for shipbuilding, waggons, flooring and telegraph poles. Karri is found in deep, loamy soils in the forty-five to sixty inch rainfall area of south-western Western Australia; this rainfall is predominantly in winter. Flowering can be from May to December.

There have been some successful plantings of *E. diversicolor* overseas, particularly in Africa. It is suitable only for high rainfall, frost-free areas, and is capable of growing five feet annually in the first ten years.

Honey produced from karri trees is regarded highly.

PLATE 26

ROSE GUM (*Eucalyptus grandis*)

On the north coast of New South Wales and in south-eastern Queensland, rose gum is found on moist, fertile soils of the valleys and on the red or chocolate loams derived from basalt. These are some of the best sites for eucalypts, bordering the rain-forest, and in some places large rose gum trees are found over-topping younger rain-forest growth. These trees may grow to 180 feet tall and six feet in diameter, with a short stocking of persistent, finely fibrous, grey bark at the base of the trunk and a long, straight, shaft-like bole, covered by smooth, powdery, white bark. The crown is moderately dense, with leaves which are glossy green on the upper surface, paler beneath.

Rose gum grows very rapidly on good sites. Height growth of ten feet per year has been recorded under natural conditions and, in plantations, even faster growth is possible. This is one of the species being planted on old farming land on the north coast of New South Wales, where, with cultivation and fertilisers, the trees are reaching as much as twenty-five feet in the first year.

It flowers from June to August.

PLATE 27

SYDNEY BLUE GUM (*Eucalyptus saligna*)

With a short stocking of persistent bark at the base of the bole, and smooth, grey bark above, Sydney blue gum closely resembles the related rose gum (*E. grandis*). In the southern part of its range this species forms a hybrid swarm with bangalay (*E. botryoides*), with some trees almost smooth-barked, others having persistent bark to the small branches. In this area, *E. saligna* is found on moderately fertile, moist soils of sheltered valleys or southerly slopes. In the more northerly areas, blue gum grows further up the slopes, until, near Brisbane, it occurs on moderately dry ridges. It is usually found on clay-loam soils, where it is often associated with tallow-wood (*E. microcorys*).

Blue gum is one of the important timbers for general use in coastal New South Wales, where it is sometimes used for flooring. It is one of the most attractive trees of the Sydney district, but is not often planted for ornamental purposes because it grows too large. It flowers from January to March.

PLATE 28

DEANE'S GUM (*Eucalyptus deanei*)

Deane's gum is closely related to the Sydney blue gum (*E. saligna*) and is sometimes mistaken for it. It occurs in the region within one hundred miles to the west and north of Sydney, and again in the area between Glen Innes in northern New South Wales and Stanthorpe in Queensland. Near Sydney it is usually found in sheltered valleys or along the streams on alluvial soils derived from sandstone, but in the MacPherson Ranges it occurs mainly on acid granite soils.

E. deanei grows to 200 feet tall and is a magnificent tree, with a long, straight bole and a dense crown. The bark is smooth throughout; it is white for most of the year, but the new bark in early summer shows patches of pale yellow and blue.

The juvenile leaves are almost circular, or broadly ovate, thin and pale green, whilst the adult leaves are rather small but usually narrower. They are pale or medium green above, and paler beneath. Cultivated trees often have larger leaves. Flowers are seen in late summer.

Deane's gum is distinguished from Sydney blue gum chiefly by the small, bell-shaped fruits with flat discs and short valves.

E. deanei was named by J. H. Maiden in 1904, in honour of Henry Deane, chief construction engineer for the NSW railways and an enthusiastic botanist.

PLATE 29

BANGALAY (*Eucalyptus botryoides*)

In eastern Victoria and along the south coast of New South Wales, often within a few yards of the beach dunes, the rather large, dense crowns of bangalay give welcome shade for holiday-makers. Although it is cut back slightly by the salt-laden winds in the more exposed sites, it is a good shelter tree, and will respond to even a little less exposure by a rapid increase in height so that the wind is swept upwards and a stand of quite tall trees is formed. Further inland, bangalay grows mainly in the valleys where it can reach 140 feet in height, on deep, moist, alluvial soils.

Bangalay has a brown, flaky-fibrous bark on the trunk, and smooth, brown or pink bark on the branches. The leaves are thick, glossy, dark green above and paler below, and the cylindrical, almost sessile fruits are carried in groups of seven on a flattened peduncle.

This species has been planted for shade and shelter, especially in coastal situations, but is also a common farm tree in western Victoria. It flowers from January to March and in spite of its coastal origin, is fairly frost-hardy in cultivation.

PLATE 30

SWAMP MAHOGANY (*Eucalyptus robusta*)

Closely related to bangalay (*E. botryoides*), swamp mahogany is also a rough-barked tree with a heavy crown of thick, leathery leaves. These are glossy, dark green above and paler below and are usually larger than those of the bangalay. The fruits are also larger, with distinct pedicels, and are usually slightly constricted just above the middle.

As its name implies, swamp mahogany occurs mainly in swamps and on the edges of coastal lagoons and rivers, where it is sometimes subjected to periodic flooding, and rarely is short of water. It is found in scattered stands, never far from the sea, from Bega in southern New South Wales to Fraser Island in south-eastern Queensland.

Although in Australia it has been used for ornamental planting only occasionally, it has been planted extensively overseas, particularly in Hawaii and northern Africa. In the humid climate of Hawaii it often produces adventitious roots from the trunk; this is one of the few eucalypts which have this ability, which may be related to its tolerance of flooded conditions. It flowers from September to November.

PLATE 31

RED MAHOGANY (*Eucalyptus resinifera*)

From the central coast of New South Wales to the area

near Maryborough in Queensland, red mahogany is found as occasional trees in the better areas of dry, sclerophyll forest. It grows on a wide range of soils, but best development is on moist but well-drained, sandy loams, where it may reach 150 feet in height. This tree, with its persistent, fibrous, red-brown bark, is superficially similar to the stringy-barks, but its leaves are quite distinct, being dark, glossy green above, paler beneath, with fine, regular venation diverging widely from the midrib. The crown is usually compact and rather dense, and, with its long, straight bole, the tree presents an attractive appearance.

Red mahogany is able to tolerate more shade than most eucalypts, but is relatively frost-tender. Its timber is strong and durable but easily worked, dark red with a rather open grain, and is popular for a wide range of purposes. It flowers from November to January.

PLATE 32

LARGE-FRUITED RED MAHOGANY (*Eucalyptus pellita*)

This tree is related to the more common red mahogany (*E. resinifera*), and is very similar in appearance, with a rough, fibrous, reddish-brown bark and thick, glossy green leaves which are paler on the under-surface.

It has a most unusual distribution; originally described from trees growing in northern Queensland, it is absent from the southern part of the State, and does not reappear until near Wyong, in central New South Wales. It occurs occasionally from there to near Bega, usually on good, loamy soils, but is also found as small misshapen trees on sandstone ridges near Broken Bay.

The most conspicuous feature of this species is the large, woody fruits, which may be up to three-quarters of an inch across. They are borne in groups of three or seven, the different numbers usually being found on separate trees, although these trees may occur in the same locality. Many species of *Eucalyptus* have flowers consistently in sevens, others have them consistently in threes, but few show the pattern displayed here.

It flowers freely from June to December.

PLATE 33

SMALL-FRUITED GREY GUM (*Eucalyptus propinqua*)

Along the eastern coast of Australia from near Newcastle north to Maryborough, the small-fruited grey gum occurs in many of the forest areas. It avoids both the heavy clays and the poorest sandy soils, but grows on a wide range of intermediate soil types, and usually on the intermediate sites, neither the best nor the worst. It is never in pure stands, and rarely the main species in an area.

This is a moderate-sized tree, rarely exceeding 150 feet in height. It usually has a long, clean bole covered by bark which is shed in large, irregular patches, leaving the surface hard and finely granular or almost smooth. When the bark is first exposed it is pale yellow or pink, but rapidly darkens to yellow or orange-pink. The colour gradually fades to light grey or fawn which eventually becomes dark grey or brown. The changing pattern of colour is one of the most attractive features of this species.

E. propinqua has a moderately dense crown of small, lanceolate leaves which are glossy green on the upper surface, paler beneath. The small, spherical or short-pointed buds usually flower in summer, and the small, hemispheric or conic fruits have a whitish skin on the disc.

PLATE 34

GREY GUM (*Eucalyptus punctata*)

Grey gum is a species which appears to have no very strong demands for growing conditions, and so it is found associated with many other species on a wide range of sites, from the sterile sandstone of the Hawkesbury to the heavier clay loams derived from shale. It seems also to be a species without strong competing ability and is usually in mixed stands with other species, or in the zone where different associations meet.

This is a very variable species, and trees of twenty or one hundred feet may be found, with large or small fruits, rounded or pointed buds, narrow or fairly broad leaves, even in relatively small areas. It is distinguished mainly by its bark, which is granular or mat on the surface rather than smooth. The bark is shed in rather large irregular patches, the new bark being bright orange, but fading to fawn or grey-brown on exposure, then darkening with age until again it is shed. The dense, dark green crown of glossy leaves which are paler on the under side, makes grey gum a good shade tree, but it seems to be generally rather slow-growing. It flowers from December to March.

PLATE 35

WOOLLYBUTT (*Eucalyptus longifolia*)

Scattered through the forest in a narrow belt along the coast from near Newcastle to the Victorian border, woollybutt is not a common, nor a very attractive tree. Its persistent, grey, finely fibrous or flaky bark and pendulous, greyish leaves give the tree a faded look, and although it may grow to over 120 feet in height, it tends to be inconspicuous in the forest. It is only when one sees the large, double-cone shaped buds hanging in threes, and the large, cream flowers in spring, that one's attention is caught, and the large, sharp-rimmed, cylindrical fruits hanging on long pedicels show that this tree is rather different. It has no close relatives, and once identified is easy to recognise again.

Woollybutt grows best on low, undulating country, or moist sandy loams, but occurs also on heavy clays derived from shale. It is rather a slow grower, but it is a useful honey tree and in its younger stages can be quite ornamental, with an irregular, heavily branched crown and pendulous smaller branches.

PLATE 36

CUP GUM (*Eucalyptus cosmophylla*)

Usually a small tree or shrub, *E. cosmophylla* occasionally grows to about fifty feet tall. It has a spreading, irregular crown of large, dull green, leathery leaves, which are broadly lanceolate or ovate, and usually curved. The bark is smooth, and shed in irregular patches to leave a grey, pink or purple surface.

Cup gum is essentially a South Australian tree, being found on Kangaroo Island and on the mainland near Encounter Bay, and in the Mount Lofty Range. It occurs on stony soils and on badly-drained sites, which has led to the use of the name 'bog gum' on Kangaroo Island.

This is an attractive, usually small tree for damp situations, with large, conspicuous flowers in winter which are usually carried in groups of three, or occasionally in fives. The flowers are followed by large, cup-shaped fruits on very short stalks.

The name *cosmophylla* means 'ornamental leaves', but the leaves are not the most attractive feature. Its attractive, coloured bark and the large flowers are also worth noticing, and it is a good tree for bees, producing both nectar and pollen.

PLATE 37

GUNGURRU (*Eucalyptus caesia*)

The common name gungurru, sometimes called gungunnu, is an aboriginal name from the Frasen Range, Western Australia, and although recorded ir most literature, the name is not widely used. The plant is more commonly referred to by its botanical name.

E. caesia is a most useful and attractive small tree up to twenty-five feet high. It grows exclusively around granite outcrops in scattered localities mainly in the southern wheatbelt area in Western Australia. Its dusty pink to red flowers from June to September, drooping, powdery, white branches, and its peculiar bark of small, longitudinally curling, reddish flakes showing a smooth, green trunk beneath make this an easily recognised species.

It is adaptable to sands and sandy loams, and will grow in some clayey soils, and it is not affected by frosts as low as twenty-two degrees F. In cultivation it is rather thin and weak, not withstanding winds easily, so that staking young trees is recommended. It can be used in cultivation where *E. ficifolia* is not suited, for it can grow in a minimum rainfall of twelve inches annually.

The name *caesia* means 'bluish-grey', a reference to the powdery appearance of the young branches, leaves, buds and fruits.

PLATE 38

LEMON-FLOWERED GUM (*Eucalyptus woodwardii*)

Potentially one of the most spectacular arid-zone trees in the world, the lemon-flowered gum grows in the Victoria Desert area of Western Australia, and near the Nullarbor Plain. It is not very common, having been collected much less than most other attractive species. It will grow in rainfalls as low as seven inches annually and will establish in sands or sandy loams.

The lemon-flowered gum attains a height of up to forty feet with a smooth, grey-brown bark and a narrow habit with an open crown. The brilliant yellow inflorescences and the fruiting capsules are heavy and cause the branches to bend, giving the tree an untidy shape. This is a feature which could be overcome when the species has been in cultivation for sufficient time for selection of more suitable forms.

E. woodwardii is already cultivated in trial plots by several councils in Western Australia, and artificial hybrids between this species and the coral gum (*E. torquata*) are being grown in a Forest Department arboretum in Kalgoorlie, and as a street tree. The species is resistant to frost and drought, and flowers between July and November.

PLATE 39

SILVER-TOPPED GIMLET (*Eucalyptus campaspe*)

The silver-topped gimlet is a slender tree which can grow to forty feet high, but is more often about thirty feet, with smooth, light bark which shows some shallow flutings. This feature, together with silvery white branchlets and a rounded crown of glaucous or blue-green foliage, is distinctive for the species. Fluted bark is also found on the common gimlet, (*E. salubris*) which is not glaucous.

E. campaspe occurs in sandy loam soils within a radius of about one hundred miles of Kalgoorlie in Western Australia, but it is not very common in any one place.

It is drought-resistant, able to grow in an annual rainfall of seven inches, is also reasonably resistant to salt, and can be cultivated in light or heavy soils. As well as being a useful ornamental tree for street planting, it is highly suitable for growing as a wind-break or for production of firewood.

The name *campaspe* is apparently a reference to the occurrence of the species on plains.

Flowering time is from November to January.

PLATE 40

STRICKLAND'S GUM (*Eucalyptus stricklandii*)

Sometimes this species is known as yellow-flowered gum or yellow-flowered blackbutt, but it seems to be known more widely by its botanical name. It occurs between Coolgardie and Norseman in Western Australia.

E. stricklandii is a tree growing up to forty feet high, but is more often seen between twenty and thirty-five feet, with a few feet of dark, rough bark at the base of the thick trunk and smooth grey and red-brown bark on the upper trunk and branches. The branchlets and buds are usually powdery white. The bright yellow flowers occur from December to January, and often continue to March. However, the buds may be on the tree for up to two years before opening.

This is a very drought- and frost-resistant species, flourishing in arid climates with rainfalls of seven to ten inches annually. It is a robust species, fast-growing and shapely. When young, its plentiful buds and thick leaves cause the branches to bend so that it may be necessary, in cultivation, to prune some of the lower branches. It may also require staking in the young stages as protection against wind. It will grow in sandy or loamy soils, and is tolerant of salt-affected soils.

Strickland's gum is suitable for street planting, as a shade tree, or as a specimen ornamental tree. It is named after Lord Strickland who was Governor of Western Australia, then of New South Wales, and later of Malta.

PLATE 41

GRIFFITH'S GREY GUM (*Eucalyptus griffithsii*)

This species is often a mallee, but sometimes a tree, occurring north, south and east of Kalgoorlie in Western Australia. The trunk has rough, grey bark, and the branches are smooth grey. The tree can grow as high as forty feet, but is more often about thirty feet.

The grey gum is a drought-resistant species, but sometimes has a crooked trunk, so that it has not been favoured by nurserymen. It is distinctive in its bark and trunk features, and by the buds being constantly in groups of three in one plane, the budcaps being hemispherical.

It occurs in red, loamy soil, often in subsaline conditions, so that it is tolerant of salt. While it has only been used for fuel and as fence posts, it could be a useful species as a windbreak, particularly in saline areas.

The grey gum is named after J. M. Griffiths who collected the specimen from which the species was first described.

Flowering time is from October to November, sometimes into December, and occasionally for several more months.

PLATE 42

COARSE-LEAVED MALLEE (*Eucalyptus grossa*)

The name *grossa*, meaning 'thick', is most apt for this unusual species, for of all the eucalypts this one is distinctive because of its large, thick, glossy leaves. It is a small mallee from six to fifteen feet high, and although its stems are not large, they are usually covered with greyish, rough bark. The branchlets and buds are reddish, and the yellow flowers from August to November are also attractive.

Drought-resistant and moderately frost-resistant, it occurs in loamy or clayey soils, and these factors make it a most useful species for many difficult inland areas. It can form an open, spreading shrub, or if pruned it can form a dense hedge plant. While slow-growing when young, it grows much faster later, and it would make an attractive and novel ornamental plant. The thick leaves colour red during frosty weather, but do not fall.

It occurs naturally south from Salmon Gums and westward to the area near Newdegate, in Western Australia.

PLATE 43

YATE (*Eucalyptus cornuta*)

Although occurring naturally in loamy, gravelly soils usually associated with granite, in the south-west of Western Australia, the yate will survive in alkaline and saline soils. It is a tree growing from thirty to sixty feet high, with dark, rough, furrowed bark on the trunk, but the branches are mainly smooth. Sometimes, for instance in the Stirling Range, a mallee form with smooth, grey stem occurs.

Characteristically, *E. cornuta* has buff-coloured, finger-shaped buds with separate, fruiting capsules. Being extremely strong, the timber has been famed as a material for wheels and shafts.

Yate will thrive under low rainfall and is frost-resistant; growth in tropical areas is even more remarkable, for it is credited with attaining heights of eight to ten feet in its first year. It is recommended for planting as ornament, shade, windbreak, or in streets and in seaside areas.

Flowers occur in January and February.

The name *cornuta* means 'horned', a reference to the appearance of the buds.

It is interesting to note that *E. cornuta* is the first Western Australian *Eucalyptus* to be named; it was first collected in late 1792 and named in 1799.

PLATE 44

WARTED YATE (*Eucalyptus megacornuta*)

The remarkable, warted budcap is an outstanding feature of this rare species. Trees in natural conditions grow up to forty feet high with smooth bark which is often somewhat mottled with patches of red and grey; the trees are erect and tend to have a thin crown of leaves. The warted yate is only known from one area in ranges about six miles east of Ravensthorpe in Western Australia where it occurs on rocky granitic soil.

Cultivated trees of this species have denser foliage with a somewhat pyramidal form, and these grow well in the coastal sands. Such plants mostly have smooth bark ranging from medium to light brown in patches, and the young twigs are red to yellow-red. It flowers in October and November.

C. A. Gardner, who discovered *E. megacornuta* in 1927, reports that it is highly regarded by apiarists. It grows in an area with an annual rainfall of sixteen inches with most of this rain falling in winter.

PLATE 45

BUSHY YATE (*Eucalyptus lehmannii*)

Fused clusters of finger-like buds and woody fruits are distinctive features of this species, and its dense, rounded, bushy form is also very typical. With branches from near ground level, mainly with smooth, grey-brown bark, and growing from twenty to thirty feet high, it is very suitable for windbreaks, shade, or ornamental planting in sandy or loamy soils. It can make about four feet of growth in two years.

The bushy yate occurs on the southern coast of Western Australia, usually on hills between King George Sound and Cape Arid. A form with larger buds and fruits occurs on Bald Island. While able to be cultivated in arid areas with rainfall of ten inches annually, it is also frost-resistant and salt-tolerant. It flowers from April to September, sometimes extending to October and November.

E. lehmannii is named after the German botanist J. C. Lehmann.

The unusual buds and fruits of the bushy yate are interesting additions to dried floral arrangements.

PLATE 46

A FORM OF THE BUSHY YATE (*Eucalyptus lehmannii* forma)

This is a further variation of the bushy yate, mainly different in having narrow leaves, smaller fruits and narrower budcaps.

Variations can occur in most eucalypt species and sometimes, as in this case, the result may be useful horticulturally.

PLATE 47

TUART (*Eucalyptus gomphocephala*)

The name *gomphocephala* means 'club-headed', a reference to the club-like buds which show the budcap distinctly wider than the calyx. These buds and the stalkless, bell-shaped fruits are unique and indicate this species precisely. The trees grow from forty to 130 feet high, with a finely fibrous or box type, grey bark throughout.

From north of Perth near Yanchep in Western Australia southward to near Busselton, the tuart grows in limestone areas, mostly being the only eucalypt in the forest which has a very open formation. The annual rainfall is from thirty to forty inches, and the area is frost-free.

Tuart timber is heavy, strong and straight, and has been used as a building material for railway wagons. The species has been cultivated successfully overseas, and is highly suitable for coastal areas with sandy or calcareous soil. It is also a useful inland species, as it is drought-resistant and moderately salt-tolerant, though needing protection from frost when young. Flowers open in March and April, a year after the buds form. Tuart, which is an aboriginal name, is recommended as a tall shade tree or street tree, and it is used in areas with a minimum of about eighteen inches rainfall annually.

PLATE 48

ROUND-LEAVED MOORT (*Eucalyptus platypus*)

Occurring naturally in heavy, grey, clayey soil, in loamy flats or moist depressions, the moort will adapt to sandy soils in cultivation. It grows between Esperance and Gnowangerup in southern Western Australia, and usually forms thickets of dense, many-branched small trees up to about twenty feet high. The bark is smooth grey, but sometimes is mottled grey and red-brown.

Quite unique are the lustrous, rounded leaves, often notched, and the compressed peduncle bearing up to nine sharply horn-shaped buds. These buds vary in length, sometimes being shortly conical, sometimes being elongated.

A variation named *E. platypus* var. *heterophylla* has leaves which are narrower than the typical form, and more lance-shaped or sometimes spathulate. This variety seems to be cultivated more than the typical form.

The moort will grow in rainfall as low as fourteen inches annually. Rain in its area of occurrence is from sixteen to twenty-seven inches annually, predominantly in winter. It is a useful species for windbreak and ornamental planting, and it is moderately frost-resistant. Flowers occur in midsummer.

The name *platypus* means literally 'broad-footed', probably a reference to the broad, rounded leaves. Moort is an aboriginal name.

PLATE 49

RED-FLOWERED MOORT (*Eucalyptus nutans*)

Because of its red flowers, *E. nutans* is sometimes more favoured as an ornamental than the closely related round-leaved moort (*E. platypus*). It grows from about four to fifteen feet high, mostly in thickets, in the area near Ravensthorpe and Hopetoun in southern Western Australia, and it occurs in sandy loam, sometimes on rocky hills.

The red-flowered moort is drought-resistant, moderately frost-resistant, and flowers from July to November. Flower colour varies from creamy to red, but only the red forms are in cultivation, where it can achieve a height of about six feet in five years, and it can also develop into a bushy shrub up to twelve feet. It will grow well in sandy loam.

Buds and fruits, up to seven in a cluster, are without individual stalks, but are borne on a flattened peduncle, and the budcaps are short, rounded, usually red. These buds are often reflexed or drooping, as expressed in the specific name *nutans* which means 'nodding'.

The red-flowered moort is a useful tan-bark species.

PLATE 50

OPEN-FRUITED MALLEE (*Eucalyptus annulata*)

A mallee growing to about fifteen feet high between Norseman and Gnowangerup in Western Australia, in cultivation this species can develop as a small tree up to twenty-five feet high. It can be identified by its mottled, grey-brown or yellowish, smooth bark, and as its common name implies, by its fruiting capsules which have strongly diverging, sharp valves giving a most open appearance. The capsules in the painting are not fully mature, with the valves still unopened.

E. annulata is a well-shaped shrub or tree which should adapt readily as a windbreak or ornamental. It usually grows in grey loamy or clayey soil, sometimes in gravelly loam, in areas with a predominantly winter rainfall of from ten to sixteen inches. It is resistant to drought and frost, and flowering occurs from July to November, sometimes until December.

The name *annulata*, meaning 'ring-shaped', refers to a free annular disc at the top of the fruiting capsule.

PLATE 51

SWAMP MALLET (*Eucalyptus spathulata* var. *spathulata*)

The narrow leaves help to distinguish the swamp mallet from other related species. It grows up to thirty feet high in heavy loam or clayey soil, sometimes near watercourses and usually in low-lying areas in the southern wheatbelt of Western Australia, north and north-west from Ravensthorpe towards Wagin. This area has an annual rainfall of from twelve to fifteen inches; the species has moderate drought- and frost-resistance. The bark is smooth, grey-brown or red-brown, and the branches project upwards from the trunk at an acute angle, giving the shrub or tree a compact appearance.

Its use for shelter or windbreaks, as well as ornament, is recommended, and it can also be used in seasonally inundated or salty areas, as much of its natural habitat is on low-lying lake fringes. It has been used extensively in windbreak planting in Victoria, where it grew to eighteen feet in four years, and in cultivation in South Australia it attained thirty feet in about thirteen years.

The term 'mallet' refers to the somewhat mallet-shaped or club-shaped fruiting capsules. The specific name *spathulata*, meaning 'spoon-shaped', refers to the very narrowly spatula-like leaves, though this shape is not a pronounced feature.

Flowering time is from October to December.

PLATE 52

TALL SAND MALLEE (*Eucalyptus eremophila*)

One of the most widespread mallees in the southern part of Western Australia, this species grows in sandy loam soil extending from about Dalwallinu eastward to beyond Kalgoorlie and southward in much of the wheatbelt. With branches from ground level, it is often up to twenty feet and sometimes as high as thirty-five feet tall with smooth, grey-brown bark. Abundant flowers from June to October can be pink or red, but bright, creamy or yellow inflorescences are most common, and the long, pointed budcaps and drooping flowers with sub-glossy leaves are distinctive for the species.

The tall sand mallee is extremely drought-resistant, able to grow in an annual rainfall of eight inches. It is also frost-resistant and will adapt to sand, sandy loams and clayey soils, and has grown successfully in a salty area. It is an exceptional species for arid-zone planting for ornament, windbreak, or as a street tree, and its suitability for such climates is given note by the name *eremophila* which means 'desert-loving'.

PLATE 53

FLUTED HORN MALLEE (*Eucalyptus stowardii*)

W. F. Blakely ascribed the common name of Stoward's mallee to this species, but neither this nor the name used above are names which are really used by people in the areas in which the plant grows.

E. stowardii occurs in loamy soils usually associated with granite rocks, with distribution restricted to a thin lens of country from Wubin to Kellerberrin. It is sometimes a mallee up to fifteen feet, but it can also be a small tree up to twenty-five feet high, with smooth, mottled bark which is light grey to brown and sometimes with a pinkish tint. When the old bark is shedding in March, new yellow-brown bark is revealed in patches.

Flutings on the bud and on the fruiting capsule are diagnostic features of the species which is named after a former Western Australian Government Botanist and Pathologist, Dr F. Stoward. Flowers are found from July to September. The species should be drought-resistant, but may not be strongly frost-resistant; however, it has not been in cultivation except in a few public gardens and little is known of its adaptation. It should be highly suitable for ornament, street planting, and perhaps windbreaks.

PLATE 54

LONG-FLOWERED MARLOCK (*Eucalyptus macrandra*)

The common name above which has been applied to this species in some literature, is rarely used. The specific name *macrandra* means 'long stamens', in this case, and indicates one of the features of the plant. The buds are long, narrow and acutely horn-shaped, and the budcap is usually at least three times as long and about the same width at the bottom as the cup or calyx tube. *E. macrandra* is very similar to the tall sand mallee (*E. eremophila*) but the budcaps on the latter are narrower at the base than the calyx tube.

This species is a free-flowering mallee with smooth bark, usually growing to about twenty-five and sometimes thirty-five feet high. It flowers from December to March, and in cultivation or in suitable conditions it may begin flowering earlier and extend a month or so later as well. It occurs as thicket in better watered situations in the Stirling and Porongorup Ranges of Western Australia, receiving up to thirty inches annually.

Because of its habit, E. macrandra makes an ideal windbreak species, and it is also an attractive ornamental, making rapid growth up to fifteen feet in five years. It is drought-resistant and moderately frost-resistant.

PLATE 55

FLAT-TOPPED YATE (Eucalyptus occidentalis)

This species is also known as the swamp yate. Both common names are suitable, as the trees do exhibit a more or less flat top to the spreading habit, and they usually grow in low-lying areas. Growing from fifty to eighty feet high, it has rough, grey bark on the main trunk and on the lower part of the branches, with smooth, silver-grey or yellow-grey bark higher up. It occurs in the southern wheatbelt of Western Australia, including coastal areas, with an annual rainfall of from sixteen to twenty inches. The bell-shaped fruits turned downwards, with strong, exsert valves, are useful in identification.

The flat-topped yate is moderately drought- and frost-resistant, and is capable of growing to nearly twenty feet in three years. It is quite suitable for growing in salty soils or in heavy, poorly-drained soils. With its attractive and plentiful flowers in late summer and autumn, E. occidentalis is a good ornamental and shade tree.

PLATE 56

SALT RIVER MALLET (Eucalyptus sargentii)

Some references apply the name Sargent's mallet to this species, but salt river mallet is far more suitable for this notably salt-resistant tree. It is usually a small tree from twenty to twenty-five feet high with a short, stout trunk covered in dark grey or black bark which exfoliates in strips; the many wide-spreading branches are smooth and brown. The leaves are narrow and shining, forming a globular crown. Further features are the narrow, horn-shaped buds on slender peduncles and pedicels, and the narrow fruiting capsules which taper down to the stalk.

E. sargentii, named after a York (Western Australia)

pharmacist, O. H. Sargent, occurs in low-lying areas or along rivers in sand or sandy loam where salt is apparent, mainly within a lens-shaped area between Cunderdin and Lake Grace in the central wheatbelt of Western Australia. Rainfall is about fifteen inches annually.

When cultivated, the salt river mallet is vigorous in growth, growing as high as forty feet, and it is capable of forming an efficient windbreak, particularly in salt-affected areas. It is moderately drought- and frost-resistant, and it flowers from October to December.

PLATE 57

BLACK MARLOCK (Eucalyptus redunca var. redunca)

This is a widespread, variable species which can be a mallee or a small to medium-height tree, perhaps up to twenty-five feet high. It grows in sandy or sandy loam soil, scattered throughout the ten to twenty inch rainfall area of south-western Western Australia.

Its features are thick, narrow, or elliptical leaves, sharply horn-shaped buds, more or less oval-shaped capsules and smooth, light and dark grey mottled bark.

E. redunca flowers from December to February and it is suitable for shade, ornament or more aptly for shelter or windbreaks.

The name redunca means 'curved backwards', a reference to the budcaps which are sometimes bent backwards when young.

PLATE 58

BLACK-BARKED MARLOCK (Eucalyptus redunca var. melanophloia)

This is similar in most characters to E. redunca var. redunca but the leaves are reputedly larger and more prominently veined and the bark is smooth and black or dark grey. Indeed, the name melanophloia means 'black-barked'.

Some botanists are agreed now that this variety really is part of the normal variation of the true species. On the other hand, in the area where such trees occur, they are usually recognised locally as being different. Such cases present difficulties in nomenclature and classification.

The recorded locality for this variety is near the Murchison and South Hutt Rivers. It could be expected that it would be suitable for windbreaks in semi-arid country.

PLATE 59

BLUE MALLET (*Eucalyptus gardneri*)

Blue mallet is a slender tree up to thirty-five feet high with grey to grey-brown smooth bark and blue-green leaves forming a dense crown. The buds are long, narrow and acute, and flowering time is during winter.

While occurring in the twelve to seventeen inch rainfall area of the southern and south-eastern wheat-belt of Western Australia, in lateritic soil, often on slopes, the blue mallet will also grow in sandy or loamy soils.

It is drought- and frost-resistant, and suitable for shade, windbreak or ornamental planting. As a farm planting species, it can provide strong timber for poles and rails, for it usually has a long, straight bole.

E. gardneri is named after C. A. Gardner, formerly the Western Australian Government Botanist.

PLATE 60

WANDOO (*Eucalyptus wandoo*)

Capable of attaining one hundred feet in height, with a bole of up to forty feet, wandoo occurs more often as a tree up to about eighty feet with a bole up to twenty-five feet. It has smooth, yellow to white bark, usually patchy, and is found on brown loam or sandy loam soils which sometimes include some gravel. Horn-shaped buds and the large tree habit make wandoo distinctive in its natural area in the fifteen to thirty inch rainfall area of south-western Western Australia. Near Toodyay it reaches its best development, but it is associated with other species of *Eucalyptus* from about Moora, north of Perth, extending in a roughly crescent-shaped area to the Stirling Range.

Wandoo is noted for its strong and durable timber and has been used in such constructions as wharves and bridges, as well as for railway sleepers, poles and flooring. In the past it has been used in wheel-making. The wood is also the basis of a tannin-extraction industry.

Wandoo is a desirable shade or ornamental tree in rainfalls such as that of its natural environment. Flowering commences in February and extends until April.

Some references list this species botanically as *E. redunca* var. *elata*. It is certainly related to *E. redunca* var. *redunca*, but there is great convenience in maintaining the two as separate species. *E. wandoo* usually grows in higher rainfall areas than other forms or varieties of *E. redunca*.

Wandoo is an aboriginal name which is widely adopted for this species.

PLATE 61

SUGAR GUM (*Eucalyptus cladocalyx*)

The tall, shapely tree with tan-coloured bark and glossy leaves, which is commonly planted on farms and roadsides in southern Australia, is not typical of the way sugar gum grows in its natural sites. Here it is more often a small, short-boled tree with a rather open crown, but on good sites it can grow to over one hundred feet with a trunk up to five feet in diameter.

Sugar gum sheds its small branchlets rather more quickly than most eucalypts and so the foliage is concentrated at the ends of the branches, and this habit, combined with the smooth bark, gives the tree an attractively clean appearance.

The juvenile leaves of this species are distinctive, being elliptical or circular, thin and green with reddish twigs. It is poisonous to stock, so that some caution is advisable in considering where to plant it. Under natural conditions sugar gum occurs on a wide topographical range, from the uplands of the Flinders Ranges to gently undulating country near sea level in South Australia. It is not widespread, however, being found only on Kangaroo Island and Eyre Peninsula in addition to the Flinders Ranges. It grows on various soil types, and is one of the few eucalypts which have been grown satisfactorily on limestone. It flowers in January and February.

PLATE 62

POWDER-BARK WANDOO (*Eucalyptus accedens*)

The powder-bark wandoo is a tree which can grow to seventy feet or occasionally higher, but is more often seen from thirty to sixty feet high. The bark is smooth, white, and powdery to the touch, this feature helping to distinguish it from wandoo (*E. wandoo*). It grows in lateritic soils, often on high or hilly ground such as in the Darling Range, and it occurs in the area from near Three Springs southward to about Pingelly in Western Australia. Sometimes it is simply known as powder bark, and it has also been called spotted gum. It flowers in summer.

Timber from *E. accedens* is hard and durable and has been used in wheel-making.

E. accedens is recommended as a shade tree for areas with a minimum rainfall of about fifteen inches annually. It is moderately drought-resistant, but would need protection from frost when young. In a twenty inch rainfall it has grown about fourteen feet in nine years, and it has been successfully planted in South Africa.

The name *accedens* means 'resembling' or 'approaching', and this was a reference to its likeness to wandoo (*E. wandoo*) in the bark, although the latter is not powdery to the touch.

PLATE 63

DESMOND MALLEE (*Eucalyptus desmondensis*)

Originally found at Mt Desmond, this species is restricted in occurrence, growing only in the Ravensthorpe Range in southern Western Australia. It is a slender, pliant shrub, rarely properly erect but often with the stems very oblique to the ground; the stems are mainly smooth, grey or white, and powdery to the touch, and may achieve a height of ten to fifteen feet.

Red, conical, cylindrical buds, creamy yellow flowers, and the flexuose habit are typical features of the Desmond mallee. It grows in stony, sloping ground on hillsides, and sometimes in clayey soil.

Flowering profusely from February to April and also sometimes in October and November, this species is an attractive and unusual ornamental, but its rather sparse foliage and thin stems do not recommend it for other purposes. It is probably moderately drought- and frost-resistant, and will flower at about four years from seed.

PLATE 64

YORK GUM (*Eucalyptus loxophleba*)

The term 'gum' is usually reserved for certain smooth-barked eucalypts, but this species is an exception as it mostly has rough, dark grey or grey-brown bark often curling off in small shreds. The amount of rough bark varies, and the upper branches are usually smooth grey to red-brown. York gum is so named because of its abundance near the town of York in Western Australia, but it is a widespread species in the south-west of Western Australia from the ten to twenty inch annual rainfall areas. It is found in sandy loam soil which is sometimes lateritic or gravelly, and can have one or several trunks, growing from twenty to fifty feet high.

Indicative of this species are the veins in the leaf, for they make a very sharp angle with the midvein and are prominent. This feature is referred to by the name *loxophleba* which means 'crooked, slanting veins'. The flowers in spring are sweet-smelling and plentiful.

York gum has also been called yandee, an aboriginal name, and it has been used in spear-making as well as in wheel-making. The timber has a hard, interlocked grain and can be worked into an attractive figure. The species is drought- and frost-resistant and is tolerant of salty soils, being a good tree for shade or shelter in shallow soils. In cultivation it can attain about forty feet or more in fourteen years.

PLATE 65

COMET VALE MALLEE (*Eucalyptus comitaevallis*)

This mallee was first found at Comet Vale, a settlement now deserted, north of Kalgoorlie in Western Australia, but it is now known to occur over a much wider area westward to near Perenjori, and probably a little distance eastward. It grows to about twenty feet in sand or sandy loam, with some dark grey, rough bark at the base of the trunks and the remaining bark smooth and grey-brown.

As with many eucalypts, the Comet Vale mallee cannot be represented fully by one illustration, for in the wide area it inhabits, it has many forms which mostly grade into one another. The budcap varies in shape, but is usually hemispherical with a small point and the rest of the bud is cylindrical. The fruits of this species are part of a panel on the Australian five dollar note.

In the past, the stems of this mallee have been used in mines as props, and although it may be a useful windbreak species, there are others more suitable. It is drought- and frost-resistant and flowers from July to September, but sometimes sporadically in other months.

PLATE 66

DUNDAS BLACKBUTT (*Eucalyptus dundasii*)

The name 'blackbutt' is used for a number of eucalypts throughout Australia, but this popular name does not indicate relationship. It usually refers, as in this case, to a stocking or butt of dark-coloured, rough bark; the higher trunk and branches of this species are richly copper-coloured. The tree habit, barrel-shaped fruiting capsules, and abruptly-pointed budcaps are features. Dundas blackbutt grows to fifty feet high, in good, loamy soil in a small area of Western Australia between Norseman, Salmon Gums and the Fraser Range, where the annual rainfall is about ten inches.

Fast-growing, under cultivation attaining up to forty feet in about fifteen years, *E. dundasii* is an excellent tree for ornament, street planting, tall windbreaks, timber and fencing. It is resistant to drought and frost. Flowering is from February to April, and in cultivation it will flower at about eight or ten feet, or within about five years of planting.

E. dundasii was named after an early mining town, Dundas, where it was found.

PLATE 67

LERP MALLEE (*Eucalyptus incrassata*)

Although known as lerp mallee in Western Australia, this species is called box or mallee box in South Australia, and yellow mallee in Victoria. A manna, called lerp by the aborigine, occurs on the leaves in the form of white threads which are clotted together by a liquid from the scale insect (*Psylla eucalypti*). The name *incrassata* means 'thickened', a reference to the thick leaves.

The lerp mallee has smooth, grey to brown stems. It can occur as thickets about seven feet high on windswept sand hills, but attains up to thirty feet in more sheltered areas. In some localities it grows near the sea coast, but also extends inland through southern Western Australia and South Australia to western Victoria.

Abruptly pointed budcaps and large, urn-shaped capsules help to identify this species.

E. incrassata is drought-resistant and moderately frost-resistant, and is most suitable for windbreaks or shelter belts, especially in very sandy soil. It is also a useful ornamental, flowering in March and April, and sometimes in October. Under cultivation it is mostly a dense mallee about twelve feet high, and it flowers at about five feet when it may be two or three years old.

PLATE 68

TWO-WINGED GIMLET (*Eucalyptus diptera*)

This tree is also known as bastard gimlet; the name *diptera* means 'two-winged', a reference to the buds and fruits which show two distinct projections which can be called wings. Often the bud seems flattened in the direction of these wings, and the buds appear directly on the stems without any stalks. These features make the species unique. However, the two-winged gimlet is a small tree usually up to about twenty feet high with a thin, yellow-brown trunk which is fluted or twisted. In this fluting, *E. diptera* is similar to the common gimlet (*E. salubris*) and the silver-top gimlet (*E. campaspe*).

The two-winged gimlet occurs only in the area of Western Australia between Norseman and Esperance, and is not markedly common in any one place. Mostly it is in red or yellow-grey soils which can be sandy loams or sometimes more clayey. It flowers in winter.

E. diptera makes an attractive small tree which could be a useful ornamental or street tree. It is drought-resistant and moderately frost-resistant, and in cultivation can grow to five or six feet in two years.

PLATE 69

PORT LINCOLN MALLEE (*Eucalyptus conglobata*)

This is a small mallee or a small tree, occurring mainly near the coast, on Kangaroo Island and from Port Lincoln on the Eyre Peninsula of South Australia across to southern Western Australia where it extends inland to near Wagin. It grows to about ten feet high, usually in sand or sandy loam, and it has smooth, grey-brown bark on thin stems. Although very similar to the Kangaroo Island mallee (*E. anceps*), it is distinguished by very short peduncles and hemispherical fruiting capsules usually about one-fifth of an inch long.

E. conglobata is not outstanding as a prospective ornamental shrub, but it may be useful in positions where salt spray or coastal sands are limiting factors for other species. In such coastal areas it could be used as an effective sandbinder or windbreak. It produces fragrantly perfumed flowers from November to February.

PLATE 70

KANGAROO ISLAND MALLEE (*Eucalyptus anceps*)

Differing slightly from the Port Lincoln mallee (*E. conglobata*) by having a broad, strap-like peduncle about half an inch long and barrel-shaped fruiting capsules, this species is very similar in other characteristics. Also, it occupies much of the same area, from Kangaroo Island and Murray Bridge, South Australia, to southern Western Australia. Its bark is smooth and grey, and it grows to about eight to ten feet high.

E. *anceps* is not a significant species, but it is a further species with the ability to grow in difficult coastal areas of sand. It would be suitable for a windbreak or sandbinder in seaside areas, and it flowers in January and February.

PLATE 71

CONGOO MALLEE (*Eucalyptus dumosa*)

Varying in most features, and growing from western New South Wales and adjacent Victoria, across South Australia to the Nullarbor Plain in Western Australia, this is also known as white mallee, and on Kangaroo Island it is known as Waikerie mallee. It grows from six to twenty-five feet high as a mallee or a small tree with rough, dark grey bark for a few feet at the base of the trunk and smooth, white bark higher and on the branches. Very short budcaps in relation to the rest of the oval-shaped buds are a feature.

Because of the variation in the plants which are at present identified as E. *dumosa*, it is not possible to depict the species fully in one painting. It may be useful as a windbreak species in arid coastal regions, as it will grow in sand and it is drought-resistant.

The name *dumosa* means 'of bushy habit', a feature which, although suitable, is not limited to this species.

PLATE 72

GILJA (*Eucalyptus brachycalyx* var. *brachycalyx*)

This is a little-known species which does not appear to have been cultivated anywhere. It occurs on the Eyre Peninsula, and in the Flinders Ranges, and eastward in South Australia. A few feet of rough bark is at the base of the stems which are smooth, grey or white above, and the species is a mallee growing up to about twenty feet high. Shining, narrow leaves, hemispherical, striated budcaps, and fruiting capsules with the valves hardly, if at all, exserted, help to distinguish gilja, which is known by this aboriginal name mainly on the Eyre Peninsula. Flowers occur in spring and early summer.

E. *brachycalyx* is drought-resistant and probably moderately frost-resistant, and could be used as a windbreak. It could also be useful as an ornamental shrub in arid zones.

PLATE 73

CHINDOO MALLEE (*Eucalyptus brachycalyx* var. *chindoo*)

This variety is now regarded as being part of the gilja (E. *brachycalyx* var. *brachycalyx*), but the painting shows the features of smaller buds and fruits which differentiate the chindoo mallee. It occurs on the Eyre Peninsula of South Australia.

If the painting of this mallee is compared with that of gilja, it can be seen that the differences are slight. It seems likely that there could be a grade completely different from one variety to the other over the area of natural distribution, and therefore it can be understood why the two are now regarded as one.

Chindoo mallee is undoubtedly a suitable wind-break species and possibly a useful ornamental in arid areas, as it is drought-resistant and probably frost-resistant, with flowers occurring in spring.

PLATE 74

CAPPED MALLEE (*Eucalyptus pileata*)

The common name is probably not used by many people, as it is merely a translation of the botanical name; *pileata* is an allusion to a close-fitting Roman cap, thus referring to the cap-like operculum.

E. *pileata* is a mallee or sometimes a small tree to twelve feet high, occurring in red, sandy loam in the south-eastern wheatbelt of Western Australia from near Southern Cross southward to Ravensthorpe, and eastward at least to the Fraser Range. In the Norseman district a form grows as a tree to about thirty feet high.

The bark is mainly smooth, grey to light brown, often with a little rough bark at the base, or the smooth bark shedding more noticeably at the base. Although the budcap varies, it is usually ribbed and broader than the calyx tube. The capped mallee flowers between December and April, mostly about January and February. It is drought- and frost-resistant, and is suitable for ornamental planting or windbreaks, or in coastal regions.

PLATE 75

KINGSCOTE MALLEE (*Eucalyptus rugosa*)

This mallee occurs in South Australia from the region around the mouth of the Murray River to Eyre Peninsula, on Kangaroo Island and extending westward along the coast. It is distinguished chiefly by the flattened peduncle, very short operculum, and usually ribbed fruits.

It appears to be salt-tolerant and a useful species for windbreaks in coastal regions, having very dense foliage, but it has not been planted widely. Flowering is mostly in summer.

The name *rugosa* means 'wrinkled', a reference to the more or less wrinkled buds.

PLATE 76

ROUGH-FRUITED MALLEE (*Eucalyptus corrugata*)

An almost hemispherical, markedly ribbed budcap and a similarly ribbed fruiting capsule, together with thick, bright green leaves on long stalks, are distinctive features of this species. The specific name *corrugata* refers to the ribbing or corrugations on the fruit and bud.

The common name, applied by W. F. Blakely, is somewhat misleading, for this species is not a mallee, but occurs as a tree up to fifty feet high, with smooth, grey to grey-brown bark and often with two to three feet of rough bark at the base. Though smooth in appearance, the bark is somewhat prickly to touch, caused by the ends of wood fibres curling slightly outwards. It grows in loamy soils which are sometimes stony or lateritic. Flowers are seen in midsummer.

E. corrugata is a tree with good form, but it has no economic use. It is drought- and frost-resistant, and is cultivated as a street tree at Coolgardie. Its natural occurrence is from about Westonia to Coolgardie, perhaps in a semi-circle connecting these two towns in Western Australia.

PLATE 77

CLELAND'S BLACKBUTT (*Eucalyptus clelandii*)

Named after A. F. Cleland, a civil engineer, and Dr J. B., now Sir John, Cleland who collected plants in much of Australia's drier country, this blackbutt has a short trunk with several feet of dark grey or black, rough bark at the base. The upper trunk and branches are smooth, grey to light brown. The budcap is ribbed but the calyx tube is smooth, and both are whitish; these features are distinctive for the species.

E. clelandii grows in red, sandy loam, attains heights up to forty feet, and occurs in an arc of country of about one hundred miles radius, north, south, and

west of Kalgoorlie in Western Australia, where the rainfall is about ten inches annually.

Flowering from September to December, and occasionally in May and June, Cleland's blackbutt may need staking when young. It is a fast-growing species which is resistant to drought and frost, and in cultivation has grown over twenty feet in ten years. Preferably it should be grown in well-drained, loamy soil, when it will make a useful tree for shade or ornament, including street planting.

PLATE 78

GOLDFIELDS BLACKBUTT (*Eucalyptus lesouefii*)

Occurring in somewhat the same area as Cleland's blackbutt, though more in the arc of country within a one hundred mile radius south and west of Kalgoorlie in Western Australia, the goldfields blackbutt can grow to sixty or seventy feet high. More often, however, it is about forty feet high with about five feet of rough, black bark at the base, and with branches being smooth, grey to yellowish or orange-coloured. It grows in red-brown, powdery loam or in sandy gravel.

Other distinguishing features are the markedly ribbed budcap and calyx tube. Flowering is mainly from October to December, but can also be intermittent for much of the year. This blackbutt is very drought-resistant, moderately frost-resistant, and mildly salt-tolerant. It is fast-growing, attaining heights of up to twenty feet in five or six years.

E. lesouefii is named after Ernest le Souef who was a former Director of the Zoological Gardens, Perth, Western Australia.

PLATE 79

JERDACATTUP MALLEE (*Eucalyptus goniantha*)

Forming a mallee from eight to twelve feet high, sometimes in grey clay or in grey, sandy, heath areas, *E. goniantha* has most distinctive, large, creamy white or pale green budcaps which can be either smooth or faintly striate, but the calyx tube is usually faintly ribbed or striate. It has smooth, greyish bark, sometimes seen to be shedding in long strips.

The name 'Franklin River mallee' has been applied to this species, as an early specimen from the collector G. Maxwell was from an area which he called the Franklin River, but such an area has not been accurately located. The name 'Jerdacattup mallee', used in some more recent references, refers to a river south-east of

Ravensthorpe, but the species occurs in a crescent of country about one hundred miles north and west from Esperance in Western Australia, and extending eastward along the coast for about eighty miles.

It is a variable species which is drought-resistant. Some forms may be moderately frost-resistant. It could be a useful low windbreak species in exposed areas, and may also make an attractive ornamental shrub. Different forms flower at different times in cultivation, one being from April to June, and another from August to October.

The name *goniantha* is a reference to the angular appearance of parts such as the fruit.

PLATE 80

CORAL GUM (*Eucalyptus torquata*)

This is also known as coral-flowered gum, Coolgardie gum, and pink-flowered gum, but is just as well known by its botanical name. The term 'gum' is usually applied to some smooth-barked *Eucalyptus* trees, but this popular species has a rough, grey bark, sometimes slightly fissured, to about ten feet, with smooth, grey branches above, reaching a total height of up to forty feet. Mainly it occurs in the area around Coolgardie, but extends southward to Norseman, in Western Australia, invariably on stony hills in red, loamy soil.

The name *torquata* means 'adorned with a collar', and this is a reference to the swollen, corrugated base of the fruiting capsule. This feature, and the ribbed, abruptly long-pointed budcap, make the coral gum easy to identify.

Flowers can be from pale pink to red, and sometimes white and, in natural stands, flowering is mainly from November to January, but can be intermittent for much of the year in cultivation.

Coral gum is cultivated widely, particularly in arid climates, where it is a popular species for street planting. It prefers a good, loamy soil, but will grow well in gravelly or sandy loam; it is certainly drought-resistant and will withstand frosts to about twenty-seven degrees F. In cultivation it grows commonly to about twenty-five feet high, with a round, spreading crown making good shade.

PLATE 81

AUGUSTA WONDER (*Eucalyptus erythronema* var. *erythronema* × *E. torquata*)

This is a hybrid which originated from the Commonwealth Railway Nursery at Port Augusta, South Australia, in the period 1946–8. The exact parentage is not known, but *E. torquata* is involved, and possibly *E. erythronema* var. *erythronema*.

Augusta Wonder is a small tree from twelve to fifteen feet high, flowering in summer. As with other eucalypt hybrids, there is no reliability at present that the original form will be reproduced unless vegetative propagation is carried out.

PLATE 82

TORWOOD (*Eucalyptus torquata* × *E. woodwardii*)

Many hybrids between the two attractive species *E. torquata* and *E. woodwardii* have been produced, using either species as the seeding parent. As yet these hybrids are unreliable, although some seedlings produce vigorous trees with similarities to both parents. Until more selection has been made, the hybrids could not be recommended in place of the parent species.

A number of these hybrids are in an arboretum maintained by the Forest Department of Western Australia at Kalgoorlie, where the cross was originated.

Flowers are seen through summer.

PLATE 83

RIDGE-FRUITED MALLEE (*Eucalyptus angulosa*)

E. angulosa is always a mallee, growing in sandy soil mainly in the southern part of Western Australia, including coastal areas, and extending to similar areas in South Australia, and then into western Victoria and western New South Wales. It grows from twelve to fifteen feet high with smooth, grey bark which sheds to a light brown or red-brown colour. The mallee is dense, thick-leaved, with a conical or sometimes pointed budcap which may be striate; the fruit is usually strongly ribbed with about ten ribs. The name *angulosa* means 'with corners', a reference to the ribs or ridges on the fruit.

The ridge-fruited mallee is ideal for shelter belts and windbreaks in dry areas, including coastal sand dunes. It is drought-resistant and moderately frost-resistant, and is tolerant of calcareous soils.

Flowers are seen from spring to summer, but may vary in different districts.

PLATE 84

SCARLET PEAR GUM (*Eucalyptus stoatei*)

The scarlet pear gum is one of the eucalypts which

are very restricted in occurrence, for it has only been found in a few places near Jerdacattup River, south-west from Ravensthorpe in Western Australia. In fact, with development for farming in the area, the scarlet pear gum may need special protection to ensure its survival in nature.

This attractive species is a compact tree with smooth, grey bark, growing to twenty or twenty-five feet high in sandy loam soil. It is easily identified by the longitudinally-ridged, pear-shaped, red buds and the similarly ridged fruits, both being pendulous and occurring only one to a stalk.

E. stoatei grows naturally in a rainfall of about sixteen inches annually, but will grow in areas with only a twelve inch rainfall. It is moderately drought-resistant and will survive light frosts. As a cultivated tree, the scarlet pear gum is most suitable for street planting, and it also has been used as a hedge; it could be used as a windbreak in either sandy or loamy soil. It can be pruned if necessary. It flowers intermittently at any time of the year.

This species was named after T. N. Stoate, formerly Conservator of Forests in Western Australia.

PLATE 85

PIMPIN MALLEE (*Eucalyptus pimpiniana*)

Collected by Henry Deane, formerly consulting engineer to the Commonwealth Railways, while inspecting the trial survey of the transcontinental railway line, on 'sandhills east of Ooldea' in South Australia, the original material consisted of mature leaves, a few fruits and a few anthers. It was described by Deane as a dwarf mallee, three to five feet high, and the native name of 'pimpin' given. This is the basis of the botanical name.

The species is undoubtedly drought- and frost-resistant, but it is still not a well-known species. It is said to flower from winter to spring.

PLATE 86

SPEARWOOD MALLEE (*Eucalyptus doratoxylon*)

Opposite leaves and drooping, creamy or greenish-white buds are useful diagnostic features of the spear-wood mallee. It usually grows to about ten feet high, but can attain fifteen feet, and it is a mallee with smooth, grey or white bark on the stems. The stems of saplings were used by aborigines who made spears, this giving a popular name for the species, and the name *doratoxylon* also refers to this aspect. W. F. Blakely used the name 'bell gum' for the plant.

Spearwood mallee occurs in sheltered parts of rocky areas in the Stirling and Porongorup Ranges, and is also found in similar scattered localities eastward as far as eighty or more miles east of Esperance, in Western Australia. It is drought-resistant, moderately frost-resistant, and should be a most attractive ornamental shrub, particularly in rocky areas near the coast. A well-drained soil is preferable.

Flowering is from August to October, but sometimes in other months.

PLATE 87

SLENDER MALLEE (*Eucalyptus decurva*)

The slender mallee is an attractive species which is highly suitable for coastal areas with low rainfall. It is moderately resistant to drought and frost, and grows naturally in sandy, lateritic soil or in sandy loam, attaining a height of up to twelve or fifteen feet. The stems are smooth, pink-grey or brown-grey, and become grey or white on shedding the old bark.

Creamy white buds and the globular fruits which hang downwards are very distinctive and are referred to by the name *decurva*, meaning 'down-curved'. Flowering is in spring.

E. decurva grows in coastal and near coastal areas of southern Western Australia. It is not common, and does not appear to have been cultivated, but would be most ornamental in gardens and could also be used as a windbreak species.

PLATE 88

SILVER MALLET (*Eucalyptus falcata*)

This has also been called white mallet. It can be a mallee or a tree up to twenty or thirty feet high, with smooth, grey or silvery, mottled bark, and grows in either gravelly soil of inland areas from Wagin to Lake Grace, or coastal sands mainly between the Stirling Range and Esperance in Western Australia. Rainfall in this area is from thirteen to eighteen inches annually, predominantly in winter. It is distinguished by its pointed, conical buds on slender stalks, and the fluted fruits; however, smooth fruits are also found in some forms.

Silver mallet has been shown to be adaptable to most soils, but it is only moderately resistant to drought and frost, probably dependent on the source of the seed. It was tried as a street tree at Kalgoorlie, an arid area, but was not highly successful.

However, where the rainfall is at least fifteen inches, the silver mallet is suitable for ornamental and windbreak planting. Under cultivation it can attain fifty feet in about fifteen yeats.

It flowers from November to December. The name *falcata* means 'curved like a sickle', and this was originally a reference to some leaves on the tree, but such a feature is not distinctive of the species.

PLATE 89

WHITE MALLEE (*Eucalyptus erythronema* var. *erythronema*)

Mostly this is a mallee up to twenty feet high, but it is sometimes a tree up to thirty feet. Smooth, mottled, powdery bark is an attractive feature, often being light and dark grey or whitish and pink, and sometimes yellowish-grey. Pendulous, red, conical buds develop into the red flowers, but sometimes naturally occurring plants have pink or white flowers. The name *erythronema* means 'red thread', referring to the filaments of the flower. As well as being called the white mallee, this species is known as the red-flowered mallee and the Lindsay gum.

The white mallee is fairly common in a more or less circular area of fifty to sixty miles radius around the town of Merredin in Western Australia, where it grows in sandy loam or in red, lateritic loam. Accustomed to a natural rainfall of ten or twelve inches annually, it is both drought-resistant and frost-resistant, able to tolerate a temperature of twenty-two degrees F.

It is an ideal street tree for arid areas, having been used in Kalgoorlie, and its free-flowering habit from October to December makes it a favoured ornamental.

PLATE 90

FLANGED WHITE MALLEE (*Eucalyptus erythronema* var. *marginata*)

The name *marginata* refers to the margin of the calyx tube which is expanded into a projecting ring around the bud and fruit in this variety. This is the only difference between this mallee and the true white mallee (*E. erythronema* var. *erythronema*). It is usually a mallee about ten feet, but sometimes up to twenty feet high, with smooth, mottled, grey, or pink and grey bark, occurring in loamy soils. Occasionally it grows in dense copses. Its main area of occurrence is in about a fifty mile radius from Pithara, in Western Australia.

The flanged white mallee flowers from October to December, and although the form illustrated has white flowers, it is also found with red or pink flowers and these are more often cultivated. It is suitable for ornamental and street planting, and is resistant to drought and frost.

PLATE 91

URRBRAE GEM (Hybrid with *Eucalyptus erythronema* var. *erythronema* as the known parent)

A probable hybrid, with *E. erythronema* var. *erythronema* as the seed parent, this form developed from a seedling of that species planted at the Waite Agricultural Research Institute in Adelaide. The original tree was about twenty-five feet high in August 1968, with a smooth, grey trunk.

Plants of urrbrae gem often have large, red flowers in summer, the filaments tipped with golden anthers. However, the seedlings from this presumed hybrid are variable and unreliable, needing great care and attention to develop a good shape.

PLATE 92

CAP-FRUITED MALLEE (*Eucalyptus dielsii*)

Named after L. Diels, formerly of Berlin Botanic Gardens, this species has an extremely restricted occurrence for a few miles around Salmon Gums, and similarly in only a small area near Ravensthorpe, in Western Australia. A projecting disc remains after flowering and becomes a reflexed, projecting rim on the fruit, giving rise to the name cap-fruited mallee.

E. dielsii is a mallee up to twenty feet, but mostly less, in height. It can also be a small tree. The bark is smooth, grey and brown in patches, or sometimes greenish-brown. The conical buds and the fruits are usually drooping, very similar to the closely related white mallee (*E. erythronema* var. *erythronema*).

Little is known of the cultivation of this rare species, but one specimen in cultivation grew to about six feet in four years. It should be frost- and drought-resistant, and is suitable for street and ornamental planting.

PLATE 93

SHE BLOODWOOD (*Eucalyptus exserta* var. *parvula*)

This species is an oddity, being closely related to the red gums, which have smooth or granular bark shed in large, irregular patches. However, it retains its bark to the small branches; it is finely fibrous, grey, and very similar to the typical peppermint bark, and this has resulted in the tree being commonly called 'peppermint'.

She bloodwood is usually only of medium size, but may reach eighty feet in height in its area of best development. This is in the Maryborough district of south-eastern Queensland where the tree is common on low-lying land. It also occurs on rather poor sites further inland and here it is usually only about forty feet tall. It has rather a compact crown of long, narrow leaves which cast only a light shade.

The name *exserta*, meaning protruding, refers to the very exserted valves on the fruit; the variety *parvula* was named because of the small size of the tree and its fruits. It is found on rocky sites in the Gayndah district of Queensland. There does not seem to be a clear distinction between the variety and the typical form, however, and the varietal name is scarcely justified. The name 'she' is a bushman's reference to the tree being not quite the same as a normal bloodwood.

PLATE 94

GREY MALLEE (*Eucalyptus morrisii*)

Occurring in the extreme south-west of Queensland, north-western New South Wales, northern South Australia, and in the MacDonnell Ranges of central Australia, this is a mallee or a small tree to about ten feet high, occasionally to fifteen feet. Rough, grey, fibrous bark peeling in strips is on the lower trunk or stems, with the upper branches smooth, dark grey.

Distinctive features are the egg-shaped buds and more or less hemispherical fruits, both virtually without stalks.

Grey mallee invariably occurs on hillsides or rocky ground, even growing near the top of some ranges up to 3,000 feet. It is undoubtedly resistant to drought and frost, but it has not been cultivated as it has no exceptional characters to recommend it as an ornamental.

E. morrisii is named after R. N. Morris who was formerly Superintendent of Technical Education in New South Wales.

PLATE 95

FOREST RED GUM (*Eucalyptus tereticornis*)

Forest red gum is the eucalypt with the greatest range of occurrence in terms of latitude, for it occurs in Gippsland, in eastern Victoria, along the whole of the eastern coast of Australia, and in Papua.

Throughout its range, this species is remarkably consistent, growing as a tree of good form, with a large, somewhat open crown. It does not typically occur in dense forest, but is usually found in more open formations, often as scattered trees on alluvial flats and stream banks, where it will tolerate heavy soils which are periodically waterlogged.

The bark of forest red gum is usually shed from the whole of the trunk and branches in irregular sheets or large flakes, leaving the surface smooth, with white, grey or bluish patches corresponding to pieces of bark shed at different times. The coppice leaves contrast with the adult ones in being large and leathery, elliptical or broadly ovate. The adult leaves are long and narrow, green on both sides, thick and glossy, with conspicuous veins.

The name *tereticornis* means 'cylindrical horn', and refers to the rather large, conic operculum which is often slightly swollen in the middle, and usually turns white or cream just before it is shed in spring when the tree flowers.

E. tereticornis was described by J. E. Smith in 1793, and is thus one of the earliest-known eucalypts.

PLATE 96

BLAKELY'S RED GUM (*Eucalyptus blakelyi*)

Blakely's red gum is typically a savannah woodland species growing with boxes and ironbarks over an extensive area along the western slopes of the Dividing Range in New South Wales, with extensions in Victoria and Queensland.

Growing in open formation, it usually has a rather short, irregular trunk and a dense, rounded crown. The bark is shed in irregular patches which vary in colour from almost white to dark grey, and as the leaves have a dull, greyish colour, the general effect is a rather sombre one. Under cultivation, *E. blakelyi* grows more rapidly and can be an attractive tree. It stands frosts, drought and wind comparatively well and is a useful tree for areas of twenty to thirty inch rainfall. It is also possibly salt-tolerant, and flowers from August to December.

PLATE 97

TUMBLEDOWN GUM (*Eucalyptus dealbata*)

On stony ridges and shallow soils, tumbledown gum grows where few other species can. It rarely grows to a big tree on such sites, and as its name implies, is usually misshapen, with a short, irregular trunk and rather open crown.

One of the distinctive features of this species is the white, waxy bloom on the branchlets, buds and fruits. It is closely related to Blakely's red gum (*E. blakelyi*) and occurs in much the same region, but on poorer sites, and is usually easy to distinguish in the field.

It flowers freely from May to October and may be useful if cultivated as a windbreak. It is also a useful species for apiarists.

PLATE 98

DWYER'S MALLEE GUM (*Eucalyptus dwyeri*)

Although this species was first described from a specimen collected at Gungal in the upper Hunter valley, it extends to the Pilliga district in the northern inland of New South Wales and also to the region between the Murrumbidgee and Lachlan Rivers.

Growing in moderately dry sites but often on very shallow or infertile soils, *E. dwyeri* is a mallee, usually about ten feet tall, with smooth, grey bark on the stems, reddish branches, and grey-green leaves. It was named by Maiden and Blakely in 1925, in honour of the Right Reverend Joseph Dwyer, Roman Catholic Bishop of Wagga Wagga, who, when parish priest of Temora, collected this species on several occasions.

E. dwyeri seems to be of little value as a timber producer but is a useful plant for bees, and has the ability to grow on dry stony ridges.

PLATE 99

CALGAROO (*Eucalyptus parramattensis* var. *parramattensis*)

First discovered on poorly-drained sites in the Fairfield district, which is now a suburb of Sydney, this species is locally common on similar sites in the arc from Mittagong through Windsor to Kurri Kurri, in New South Wales. It is able to tolerate periodic flooding and so can persist on these spots in spite of being only a small tree which would be rapidly overtopped in the surrounding forest.

E. parramattensis has a dull, pinkish-grey bark, with a smooth to granular surface, which is shed in irregular sheets, giving a patchy appearance to the trunk, somewhat similar to the grey gums. It is more closely related to the red gums, however, as is shown by its fine, dull green leaves which are the same colour on both surfaces and have rather irregular venation.

This tree can be quite attractive, with its pink-toned bark and fine foliage. Its ability to grow in periodically wet sites makes it a useful species for ornamental planting on such sites and, because it does not grow too large, should be used more often than at present.

Calgaroo flowers from November to January.

PLATE 100

ROUND-BUDDED CALGAROO (*Eucalyptus parramattensis* var. *sphaerocalyx*)

This variety is occasionally seen with the more typical form of calgaroo (*E. parramattensis* var. *parramattensis*), and it was first described from the same general locality, so there seems to be no real justification for keeping it separate.

However, the painting illustrates the distinguishing feature of rounded, instead of pointed, buds. The varietal name *sphaerocalyx*, meaning spherical calyx, also refers to this feature.

Flowering time and other features are the same as for calgaroo.

PLATE 101

ORANGE GUM (*Eucalyptus bancroftii*)

E. bancroftii can grow to a rather tall, well-formed tree, but is frequently short-boled and misshapen, with a spreading crown. Perhaps its most attractive feature is the bark which, although not as smooth as in many of the gums, is more colourful than most. The irregular patches of dark and light grey are mixed with patches of orange and red, brightest in mid-summer and gradually fading during the winter, to be replaced the following year.

Orange gum is common on poorly-drained, alluvial soils along the coast of northern New South Wales and southern Queensland but it also occurs on sandy soils, and in the New England district of New South Wales is found on rocky ridges and hillsides, growing in poor, granitic soils.

The rather long, angular, outer operculum is often retained until the buds are quite large, so that when it is shed, the inner operculum has a distinctive appearance, like an elongated acorn. Flowering is irregular, the flowers are rather small and not conspicuous amongst the dark green foliage.

In the region west of Tenterfield there is a tree which is generally regarded as a form of *E. bancroftii*, but it has grey-green leaves. This is the form pictured.

Eucalypts, plates 98–101 • 33

Orange gum was named in honour of Thomas Lane Bancroft, who collected specimens of some Queensland eucalypts.

PLATE 102

RIVER RED GUM (*Eucalyptus camaldulensis*)

One of the most widespread eucalypts, the river red gum occurs in the arid and semi-arid areas of the Australian mainland, taking in rainfall zones from about five to twenty-eight inches annually. Gum leaves which have been depicted on many Australian postage stamps have been of this species. Being so typically Australian, and yet perhaps not seen by the majority of the coastbound population, it is also a strange fact that this species was first described in literature from a cultivated tree in the garden of the Camalduli religious order in Naples, Italy.

The bark is smooth, white or grey, and often streaked with red. Trees grow to one hundred feet, and are mostly restricted to the banks of rivers which have only seasonal or intermittent flows. The crown is dense. There is much variation in the buds which range from egg-shaped to conical or beaked; the fruit is typically small with protruding, triangular valves. Flowering is in September and October.

River red gum is quite adaptable from sandy to heavy soils, is drought- and frost-resistant, slightly salt-tolerant, and able to withstand periodic inundation. It is extremely fast-growing and can attain up to sixty feet in ten years under a ten inch rainfall. The usefulness of river red gum as shade, highway planting, ornamentals, timber, windbreaks when kept cut, or as a lawn tree with grass to the trunk is confirmed by its being the most widely planted eucalypt in the world.

PLATE 103

FLOODED GUM (*Eucalyptus rudis*)

Very closely related to the river red gum (*E. camaldulensis*), the flooded gum of Western Australia actually continues its distribution where the river red gum ceases. It occurs in the strip of coastal Western Australia south of Geraldton to the vicinity of Bunbury and extends inland for sixty to eighty miles. In the area from about Geraldton to Jurien Bay there appears to be some intergrading with the river red gum.

Invariably, the flooded gum is associated with watercourses, and usually has a short, stout trunk with rough, dark grey bark and with the upper branches smooth and grey. It grows to about sixty feet. The buds and fruits are difficult to distinguish from those of river red gum, but usually the rim of the fruit of flooded gum is shorter and flatter than that of river red gum; the buds are larger with a bluntly conic operculum.

Flooded gum is sometimes known by the aboriginal name of 'moitch' in Western Australia.

The name *rudis* means 'rough, unused, or raw', and may apply to the basal, rough bark, or perhaps to the timber which is only suitable for fuel. Flowering time is September and October.

This species can provide useful shade, but it has not been cultivated much in Australia, as other species are more suitable. It has, however, been cultivated in other parts of the world, growing to twenty-five feet in six years in a thirty inch rainfall in Algeria. Its resistance to frost is moderate, but it is unlikely to survive heavy or consistent frosts.

PLATE 104

SNAPPY GUM (*Eucalyptus brevifolia*)

Snappy gum is a small tree up to twenty-five feet, but usually less in height. It is a marked feature of the twelve to twenty-five inch rainfall area of the Northern Territory and north-western Queensland, being more dominant in the lower rainfall range of this area. The tree occurs on some small, spinifex, lateritic sandplains north of Tennant Creek, and more typically on rocky hills where it is recognised by its smooth, white trunk and small, dull, grey-green leaves. Some specimens, such as in the painting, show longer leaves, however.

Though somewhat straggly in growth in its natural habitat, *E. brevifolia* would probably grow more erect in cultivation. It is drought-resistant, but susceptible to frosts, yet if protected for a few years when young it would probably survive moderate frosts. With its smooth white trunk and small stature, it could be a most useful small tree in arid or semi-arid areas, possibly growing well in higher rainfalls, also.

Flowers occur in spring and summer. The timber is used for fencing.

The name *brevifolia* refers to the normally short leaves of the species.

PLATE 105

WHITE GUM (*Eucalyptus alba*)

This is one of the few species of *Eucalyptus* which

occur in areas outside Australia. It occurs in nor-thern Australia from Western Australia to Queens-land where it extends down the coast, and it also grows in southern New Guinea, Timor, and some adjacent islands. Considering the wide area in which it occurs, variation could be expected; there is so much variation that there have been different botanical and common names for different forms. Some of the common names are ridge gum, white gum, mottled gum, wongoola, poplar gum, and khaki gum.

E. alba can be a tree to sixty feet, but it is sometimes much smaller, with smooth, white to salmon-pink bark, growing on flat country and also on hillsides and ridges. Prominent veins in the leaves, which are partly deciduous, and thin-rimmed, fruiting capsules, are distincitive features. Its bole is about half the height of the tree.

White gum grows mainly in a monsoonal rainfall of from thirty to sixty inches annually, and it is found from sea level to about 1,400 feet above sea level. It has made growth of fifteen to twenty feet in three years in cultivation in Fiji, and it has been cultivated in other tropical countries. Flowering generally occurs between May and August

PLATE 106

SWAMP GUM (*Eucalyptus ovata*)

Swamp gum is one of the few species of eucalypt which can stand 'wet feet'. It is able to grow on areas which are regularly flooded for several months of the year and is usually the only tree on such areas. It is not confined to swamps, however, being found on a wide range of sites, from exposed coastal plains to mountain foothills.

This tree is widely distributed in northern and eastern Tasmania and occurs in scattered localities from Kangaroo Island, through the southern and eastern parts of Victoria and the cooler parts of south-eastern New South Wales. With a dark grey, rather scaly bark on the lower trunk, and smooth, pinkish bark on the branches, it is a distinctive, but not always a very attractive tree. The rather dense crown of glossy, dark green leaves gives cool shade and makes swamp gum a useful tree for farm planting, especially on badly-drained sites.

The double-conic buds are borne in groups of seven, and produce cream flowers in winter and spring, to be followed by conic fruits with a flat disc.

The name *ovata* refers to the oval-shaped leaves

which were on the specimen originally described. With later collections, however, it was found that the leaves varied from oval to narrowly lanceolate.

PLATE 107

BROAD-LEAVED SALLY (*Eucalyptus camphora*)

E. camphora is closely related to E. ovata and, like that species, is known as swamp gum, and can grow in areas which are periodically flooded. This species is found in colder areas than E. ovata, being usually restricted to upland swamps, between Rylstone, in New South Wales, and eastern Victoria, and at altitudes up to about 4,000 feet, where snow may lie on the ground for weeks each winter.

R. T. Baker separated this species from E. ovata on differences of leaf shape, fruit size, and bud shape, this species having broader, typically blunt leaves, small fruit, and an operculum longer than the calyx.

E. camphora is usually a small, crooked tree with rough, hard, flaky bark at the base of the trunk, and lead-coloured or dark grey bark on the upper part. The small, cream-coloured flowers are inconspicuous when they appear in autumn, and the tree is not out-standing as an ornamental.

PLATE 108

BLACK GUM (*Eucalyptus aggregata*)

E. aggregata is not a common tree naturally. It occurs on the central and southern tablelands of New South Wales, and has been recorded from Victoria but is rare in that State.

Growing in cold, damp situations, often in frost hollows, black gum must be regarded as a very useful tree for stock shelter. It is hardy to frost and wind, and although it is usually only a small tree, it is sufficiently attractive to warrant its use as an orna-mental. The crown is dense, dark green, with rather small, narrow leaves.

The bark of black gum is persistent to the twigs. It is finely fibrous to flaky, dark brown or almost black, and with the dark foliage, the tree gives a sombre appearance. The small, ovoid buds flower in summer, and the small, hemispheric fruits with a raised disc and protruding valves are distinctive.

The name *aggregata*, meaning 'clustered', refers to the way that the fruits are borne in umbels of seven, on short pedicels.

PLATE 109

NARROW-LEAVED BLACK PEPPERMINT (*Eucalyptus nicholii*)

One of the most attractive rough-barked trees, *E. nicholii* has been planted for ornamental purposes both in Australia and overseas. It is especially popular in California where its fine, light green foliage and rounded, compact crown are much admired, and the pink to plum-coloured tint of the new leaves is used as a background to floral displays.

In contrast to its attractive showing as a garden specimen, *E. nicholii* is an inconspicuous, rather poorly-shaped tree in its native state. It does not usually grow to more than forty feet, with a short bole covered by fibrous, brown bark and rather irregular branches with a tendency towards a weeping habit.

The many, small, creamy flowers in autumn are borne in groups of seven, along the branches. The fruits are also small and hemispheric with a flat or slightly raised disc.

E. nicholii occurs naturally on shallow soils overlying slates, but will grow on a wide range of soils. It is frost-hardy and moderately drought-resistant.

The narrow-leaved black peppermint is more often simply known by its botanical name; it was named after Richard Nichol, formerly a chief clerk at the Sydney Botanic Gardens.

PLATE 110

WALLANGARRA WHITE GUM (*Eucalyptus scoparia*)

On the tops of the granite hills around Wallangarra, and on both sides of the nearby border between New South Wales and Queensland, grows a slender tree, thirty to forty feet tall, with a smooth, white bark and a light, open crown. This is the Wallangarra white gum. The name *scoparia* means 'broom-like', a reference to the slender habit of the tree.

It is not a well-known species and occurs naturally in a very limited area. It is very similar to manna gum (*E. viminalis*) in general appearance and has long, narrow leaves of shining, green colour and faint venation, and the small buds and fruits are produced in umbels of seven, similar to the northern form of manna gum. The flowers are seen in summer.

The juvenile leaves are distinctive, tapering to the petiole rather than being rounded at the base.

PLATE 111

BRITTLE GUM (*Eucalyptus mannifera* ssp. *maculosa*)

This is undoubtedly one of the best trees for planting in cool climates. It grows rapidly in early years, but slows by the time it is about twenty feet high, except on very good sites, and retains its graceful form for many years.

The smooth, white bark is covered by a powdery bloom; in summer the bark turns pink and, where the bloom is rubbed off, bright red, before it is shed in large sheets to leave a new, pale cream surface. The fine, grey-green leaves shed a light shade and allow the graceful form of the branches to show through. The small, cream-coloured flowers from spring to summer, and small, rounded fruits add to the impression of lightness, although occasionally, trees planted on very fertile sites produce heavy crops of fruit.

Brittle gum is common on shallow, well-drained soils of the southern tablelands of New South Wales.

It will grow on rocky hillsides, where there is scarcely any soil, but of course on such sites it is a small, irregularly-shaped tree. Often in such places it is associated with one of the scribbly gums (*E. rossii*) and these two species, with smooth, cream or white bark and fine, greyish foliage, may be very difficult to distinguish.

PLATE 112

APPLE-TOP BOX (*Eucalyptus angophoroides*)

The word *angophoroides* means 'like an *Angophora*', and this species, like apple box (*E. bridgesiana*), resembles the rough-barked apple (*Angophora floribunda*), particularly in the bark, which is light brown to grey-brown, soft and friable. Apple-top box is closely related to apple box and resembles it in some features, but while apple box is mainly an inland species, apple-top box is confined to the coast of New South Wales and eastern Victoria.

It could be expected to be less frost-resistant than *E. bridgesiana*, but it has seldom been planted outside its area of natural occurrence, so its hardiness has not been sufficiently tested. It flowers from spring to early summer.

PLATE 113

APPLE BOX (*Eucalyptus bridgesiana*)

Apple box is a useful tree for shade and shelter and has

been planted for ornamental purposes, although it is not as popular as some of its smooth-barked relatives. It is also useful as a honey tree, flowering regularly and profusely in autumn. It occurs over a wide area of south-eastern Australia, on the western side of the Dividing Range from northern New South Wales to Victoria, where it extends to the coast in the Gippsland region.

The name apple box refers to the similarity of this tree, and particularly the bark, to the rough-barked apple (*Angophora floribunda*). The bark is light brown or grey-brown, persistent to the small branches, soft and friable. It also tends to be ridged or flaky.

Apple box is usually a woodland tree, with a short bole and large crown. The leaves are long and narrow, bright green, usually with yellowish twigs. In contrast, the juvenile leaves are heart-shaped, with crenulate margins and silvery-grey surfaces, and are arranged in not quite opposite pairs along the stem.

This species is frost-resistant and moderately hardy to drought. It prefers moist sites and is usually found on the lower slopes, on fairly deep loams or clay loams.

E. bridgesiana is named after F. Bridges who was the Chief Inspector of Education in New South Wales during part of the late nineteenth century.

PLATE 114

TENTERFIELD WOOLLYBUTT (*Eucalyptus banksii*)

Named by Maiden in 1904 to honour Sir Joseph Banks who came to Australia with Captain Cook, and whose name is commemorated in the genus *Banksia*, this species is a medium-sized tree, usually rather crooked in growth. It is found on granite hills in the tableland country near Tenterfield and Wallangarra, and on the border between New South Wales and Queensland.

Tenterfield woollybutt, as the name implies, is a tree with persistent, sub-fibrous bark on the trunk, and smooth branches. The bark on the trunk is dark grey, woolly or fuzzy to touch but rather smooth on the surface, intermediate between a gum and a box type.

E. banksii is related to the apple box (*E. bridgesiana*) but occurs more on hills than that species. It also has larger foliage and large, green rather than glaucous, juvenile leaves, while the small, slightly angular buds and the small, hemispheric fruits are sessile. Flowers occur in late summer.

PLATE 115

BUNDY (*Eucalyptus goniocalyx*)

This tree is very similar in general appearance to the apple box (*E. bridgesiana*), but usually grows on drier sites. It is mainly a tree of intermediate altitudes, extending from the higher country in western Victoria to the tablelands of New South Wales, where it grades into a related species, mealy bundy (*E. nortonii*).

Bundy is usually a small, rather misshapen tree, with spreading branches and long, strap-shaped leaves which are dull grey-green on both surfaces. The bark is soft, sub-fibrous, and irregularly cracked and ridged. *E. goniocalyx* is distinguished from *E. bridgesiana* chiefly by its buds, which are sessile, elongated and angular, and by the fruits which are also sessile and cylindrical.

The shape of the buds is referred to in the name *goniocalyx* which means 'angled calyx'. This species flowers in late autumn.

Although not a good timber-producing tree, bundy is useful for shade and shelter, particularly because of its ability to grow on bare, rocky hillsides. It is drought-resistant, and able to withstand moderate frosts.

PLATE 116

MEALY BUNDY (*Eucalyptus nortonii*)

In 1917 the French botanist M. Trabut described a species of *Eucalyptus*, based primarily on a watercolour painting by Cordier, but including also a specimen which he photographed. This species, which he named *Eucalyptus cordieri*, was therefore based on mixed material, for Cordier's painting appears to be of a hybrid with three-flowered inflorescences, whilst the photograph is of a seven-flowered plant.

W. F. Blakely took up the name *E. cordieri* and applied it to a tree growing in Australia, the mealy bundy, which is closely related to *E. goniocalyx*. More recently, however, it has been recognised that this was not the original *E. cordieri* and L. Johnson gave a new name, *E. nortonii*, based on the name of a variety of *E. cordieri*, and named it after E. A. Norton who collected the original type specimen.

E. nortonii occurs on the tablelands of New South Wales, extending to the inland slopes of the Dividing Range of eastern Victoria. There is a gradual change, from north to south, from a form with large flowers and fruits to one with much smaller parts, much like those of *E. goniocalyx*. The main distinguishing feature is that the buds and fruits of *E. nortonii* are covered by a waxy, whitish bloom.

This is a short-boled, sprawling tree with a rough, light brown, more or less scaly bark and large pendulous leaves, flowering in spring. It grows on rocky hillsides, at intermediate altitudes, and is frost-resistant.

PLATE 117

MANNA GUM (*Eucalyptus mannifera* ssp. *mannifera*)

The name and description of *E. mannifera* were published by Mudie in 1834, from material collected by Alan Cunningham in 1824 at Bathurst, but the application of the name was later confused, and various races of this rather variable species were given separate names. More recently, L. Johnson has united them as subspecies of *E. mannifera*. The name *mannifera* means 'manna-bearing', referring to the substance which exudes from the leaves when they are damaged.

The type race, with moderately broad leaves, is widespread on the central tablelands of New South Wales, and similar forms occur in the western part of the southern tablelands and the south-western slopes. It intergrades with other subspecies, so that there is no clear line of demarcation between them.

E. mannifera is a tree of moderate size, with a smooth, white bark which is covered by white, powdery bloom. This rubs off in places, leaving greenish patches. The bark changes colour in midsummer, especially on the side of the trunk exposed to the sun, becoming orange-red, just before it is shed in large sheets. Flowering occurs in summer.

The leaves are lanceolate and dull green, with fine, faint venation. The crown is rather sparse, so that the tree casts only a light shade.

PLATE 118

CANDLE BARK (*Eucalyptus rubida*)

E. rubida is named for the red colour which develops in the bark, especially on the sunny side of the tree in midsummer. This bark is shed over the whole surface of the trunk and branches, leaving a smooth, powdery, white surface. Sometimes the bark from the branches hangs in long ribbons, and the tree is sometimes known as ribbon gum.

This tree is closely related to the mountain gum (*E. dalrympleana* ssp. *dalrympleana*) and occurs over much the same range, from the northern tablelands of New South Wales to south-eastern Tasmania. It is found on topographically lower sites than the mountain gum, usually on rather cold, damp sites.

It is generally a small to medium-sized tree with a straight bole and a rather light crown of grey-green leaves. The twigs and buds are often covered by a white, waxy bloom and the juvenile leaves are also waxy; they are usually almost circular or notched at the top, but the intermediate leaves are sometimes ovate and pointed.

E. rubida is frost-hardy but only moderately drought-resistant. It is an attractive tree and is often planted for ornamental purposes, flowering in summer. Unfortunately it is frequently attacked by leaf-eating beetles. It is also marked on the trunk by horizontal scars which appear to be caused by a bark beetle.

PLATE 119

MOUNTAIN GUM (*Eucalyptus dalrympleana* ssp. *dalrympleana*)

E. dalrympleana was named by J. H. Maiden in honour of Richard Dalrymple Hay, former Chief Commissioner of Forests in New South Wales. It is one of the most attractive of our highland eucalypts, although usually only of moderate size, being generally less than 120 feet tall, and about four feet in diameter. Its clean, white bark and shining, light green leaves present a very pleasing picture in the clear, mountain air of south-eastern New South Wales and the adjacent Victorian Alps, or the central highlands of Tasmania.

This is a species which will stand quite heavy falls of snow and long winters, although the summers are mild and rainfall is usually reliable, with an annual range of thirty-five to fifty-five inches, most of which falls in the winter. In Tasmania, mountain gum occurs at altitudes of 1,000 to 3,000 feet, but on the mainland the range is 2,000 to 4,500 feet. Usually the sites are well-drained although rarely dry.

Mountain gum is closely related to candle bark (*E. rubida*) but generally occurs on higher, steeper sites; these two species are difficult to distinguish, but mountain gum shows less tendency to have red bark in summer, and the intermediate leaves tend to be more pointed. Candle bark has waxy twigs and buds whilst those of mountain gum are green.

This species is normally three-flowered, but on the northern tableland region of New South Wales a seven-flowered form occurs. This has been regarded as a separate subspecies known as *E. dalrympleana* ssp. *heptantha*.

Flowering occurs in late summer.

PLATE 120

TINGIRINGI GUM (*Eucalyptus glaucescens*)

This species was originally described as a small tree, but more recently, specimens which appear to be closely similar have been collected from trees up to 170 feet tall. The name *glaucescens* refers to the glaucous, or dusty grey, parts of the tree.

Tingiringi is a small town on the mountains near the border between New South Wales and Victoria, one of the localities for this species. It appears to be restricted to mountains, at about 4,000 feet altitude, from just south of Canberra to the Baw Baw Range in southern Victoria.

Apart from the silver-grey to glaucous foliage, *E. glaucescens* is distinguished by the shape of the buds, which are borne in groups of three and are cylindrical with a short operculum which is flatly conic, or like an inverted saucer, with a small, central point. In the larger form, from near Mt Erica in Victoria, the leaves are alternate and stalked, and are lanceolate with a rather narrow point.

Tingiringi gum is one of several mountain species, with silver leaves, which are useful for ornamental planting. Its smooth bark is shed in reddish flakes, leaving a white, powdery surface. The flowers appear in late summer or autumn.

PLATE 121

SPINNING GUM (*Eucalyptus perriniana*)

This species was first discovered by G. S. Perrin, and the name given to it in his honour by Ferdinand von Mueller in 1890, but the formal publication of this name was done by Rodway in 1893.

The most outstanding feature about this species is that the juvenile leaves are joined at their bases to form a single, elliptical blade. The adult leaves are normally rather narrow and stalked. All are glaucous, so that the tree is rather attractive. It is usually less than twenty-five feet tall and rather irregular in form, with a smooth, blotched or scaly bark at the base of the trunk.

Spinning gum occurs in isolated patches in Tasmania, Victoria and New South Wales. In Tasmania it is found in wet hollows on poor, mudstone soils at altitudes of 1,000 to 2,000 feet whilst in Victoria and New South Wales it occurs on the high mountains, between 4,000 and 6,000 feet. It is thus a distinctly cold-climate species, but grows well in cultivation in much warmer, drier localities. Many of the leaves, as they die, become detached from the stem but form discs which rotate in the wind. This is the origin of the common name.

E. perriniana produces white flowers in late summer.

PLATE 122

BOOKLEAF MALLEE (*Eucalyptus kruseana*)

Also recorded in some publications as Kruse's mallee, *E. kruseana* is perhaps better known by its botanical name which honours John Kruse of Melbourne. It has become a popular species for cultivation, particularly in dry climates, for it will grow in an eight inch rainfall.

The bookleaf mallee occurs naturally as a small, straggly mallee, or occasionally a small tree, up to about ten feet, but more usually six to eight feet. It occurs only in the vicinity of granite rocks in several isolated areas, including the Fraser Range, near Karonie, and near Binyarinyinna Rock, in Western Australia. The bark is grey-brown to yellow-brown and smooth.

In its natural habitat flowering is from April to June, but in cultivation it may bloom for longer periods, up to November.

Reasons for the popularity of this species are its grey-blue leaves which are opposite and rounded, without stalks, and the pointed, conical buds which are mostly pink, followed by the yellow flowers. In cultivation, it can become an upright shrub with a single stem; it should be pruned only lightly. It is drought- and frost-resistant, though repeated frosts may damage young plants. It will grow in sandy or loamy soil, making an excellent ornamental or a useful small street tree.

PLATE 123

Eucalyptus brachyphylla

Occurring in much the same restricted localities as the bookleaf mallee (*E. kruseana*), near Karonie and near Binyarinyinna Rock in Western Australia, this species differs mainly in having stalked leaves. It is either a straggly mallee or a small tree to about ten feet high, with smooth, grey-brown to yellow-brown bark which can sometimes be slightly rough at the base of the thin stem. It is only found in the vicinity of granite rocks.

Flowering is mainly in the period from May to July, but in cultivation can extend earlier or later in rainfalls which are higher than its native eight or nine inches annually.

E. brachyphylla could be a useful small tree or shrub in ornamental or street planting, for its grey-blue foliage is an attractive feature, but it is not preferred when *E. kruseana* is available.

The botanical name means 'short-leaved' which is certainly applicable in comparison with the full range of eucalypts, but the name is, perhaps, inapt in comparison with its very close relative *E. kruseana*, which has even smaller leaves.

PLATE 124

SILVER GUM (*Eucalyptus crenulata*)

In 1938 this small (up to thirty feet tall) glaucous tree was discovered in wet, marshy ground in the Acheron Valley which runs through the mountains to the north-east of Melbourne. This species is similar to the Tasmanian silver gum (*E. cordata*), but has smaller, stalked leaves which are shining green on the upper surface, white beneath, and heart-shaped with crenulate margins, and smaller buds and fruits. The buds usually are egg-shaped with a narrow, distinct beak at the apex, and are borne in umbels of up to nine, in the axils of the upper leaves.

The small stems of this tree are covered by thin, grey or grey-brown bark, with horizontal bars of white.

The tree has been planted for ornamental purposes in a few localities in Victoria and makes an attractive garden specimen, flowering in spring. It is recommended for cold, wet sites.

PLATE 125

POWDERED GUM (*Eucalyptus pulverulenta*)

This is a species which grows naturally in only a few isolated places in the central and southern tablelands of New South Wales, but is cultivated on a large scale in California, where the young shoots are used extensively in the cut flower trade. Particularly desirable forms, with small leaves and an intensely silver bloom, are in much demand. In Australia, it is not used commercially in this way, but it has been planted as an ornamental tree, and has achieved some popularity because of its unusual form, its attractive

bark, and stiff, silvery leaves. It is also sometimes called the silver-leaved mountain gum.

The silvery leaves are heart-shaped, sessile and borne in pairs along the branches, which often assume horizontal attitudes or branch more or less at right angles. The flowers, in spring, are borne in groups of three, in the axils of the leaves; flowering is often profuse, and the branches have successive lengths carrying buds, flowers, new and old fruits.

The bark of *E. pulverulenta* is shed in small flakes, leaving a smooth, reddish surface on the trunk, whilst the branches are white or greenish and covered by a waxy bloom.

E. pulverulenta was first described by Sims in 1819 from a specimen cultivated in an English nursery. Since the locality where it grows naturally could not have been discovered before 1813, when the Blue Mountains were first crossed, seeds must have been sent to England by one of the first explorers of the area. The botanical name means 'powdery', a reference to the silver bloom on the leaves and twigs.

PLATE 126

BELL-FRUITED MALLEE (*Eucalyptus preissiana*)

Named after Ludwig Preiss, a botanist of the Hamburg Museum, who visited Western Australia for four years from 1838, this species is found from the Stirling Range area to near Esperance in Western Australia. It grows in poor, stony, clayey, or lateritic soil, being a straggly or spreading shrub with smooth or mottled grey bark; mostly it is from four to six feet high, but it can sometimes grow to fifteen feet.

The large, conical buds occur in threes, without stalks, and after flowering the fruit becomes large, woody and distinctively bell-shaped. Obtuse, thick leaves are also typical.

Although in its natural habitat rainfall is from sixteen to twenty inches annually, the bell-fruited mallee may withstand lower rainfalls. It is resistant to frosts to about twenty-four degrees F.

Flowering is from July to October, and the blooms last well as cut flowers.

PLATE 127

BULLICH (*Eucalyptus megacarpa*)

Distinctly hemispherical fruits with a prominent rim or ring, and the top-shaped buds are identifying features of this species, which was early called blue gum because of a likeness to the Tasmanian blue gum (*E. globulus*).

Bullich is a tree up to eighty feet high, growing in low-lying, moist ground in the south-west of Western Australia where the annual rainfall is from thirty to forty inches. The bark is smooth and white to yellowish-white, deciduous in small flakes. Timber of this species has little value, but the mature trees can provide excellent shade.

Adequate water is essential for good growth of bullich, and it is probably frost-sensitive. It flowers in October and November.

The name *megacarpa* means 'large fruit', and while the species does have a large fruit, it is not as large as that of some other species of *Eucalyptus*.

PLATE 128

CROWNED MALLEE (*Eucalyptus coronata*)

The strongly ribbed buds and the rounded protuberances in the top of the fruit are diagnostic features of the crowned mallee. It grows in rocky ground on hills near the south coast of Western Australia, principally on the Middle and East Mt Barren ranges. A height of five to six feet is its maximum in natural conditions, but it becomes taller in cultivation.

Flowering in July and August, *E. coronata* is a useful and unusual garden shrub, and the buds provide excellent material for flower arrangements.

The specific name *coronata* means 'crowned', a reference to the crown-like appearance of the fruit.

This mallee has been used for windbreaks in Victoria. It is moderately drought- and frost-resistant.

PLATE 129

TASMANIAN BLUE GUM (*Eucalyptus globulus*)

The Tasmanian blue gum is certainly the best-known Australian tree in California and in Spain. Many other countries are growing this species, and it is renowned for its rapid growth. Blue gum was introduced into California in 1853 by a Mr Walker, and extensive planting was encouraged in the period 1886–1900, with the idea of establishing woodlots for the production of both lumber and firewood. Unfortunately, this species is not well suited for either purpose, and the venture was not very successful. Nevertheless, *E. globulus* is still a major feature of the landscape from Los Angeles to San Francisco, and many Californians believe it to be a native tree.

One of the few eucalypts which bear their buds and fruits singly, Tasmanian blue gum is most easily recognised by these. The bud is large, warty and usually has a waxy bloom. The fruit is broadly top-shaped, with a wide, flat disc. This tree, like the closely related southern blue gum (*E. bicostata*) is a coarse tree, with large, leathery leaves, heavy branches, and dense crown. The juvenile leaves also are distinctive, being opposite, stem-clasping, ovate and glaucous, and carried on a four-winged stem.

Tasmanian blue gum occurs in small areas in the Otway Range and Wilson's Promontory in Victoria, and on islands in Bass Strait, but its optimum development is in the south-east of Tasmania, where it grows on moist loams to clays, and may reach 180 feet in height.

The large, cream-coloured flowers appear in spring, and provide moderate quantities of nectar.

PLATE 130

SOUTHERN BLUE GUM (*Eucalyptus bicostata*)

Like its close relative, the Tasmanian blue gum (*E. globulus*), southern blue gum grows best on moist, rather heavy soils on moderately hilly country. Its principal occurrence is in Victoria on the northern slopes of the Australian Alps, but smaller areas occur in Gippsland and western Victoria, and in southern New South Wales. Sometimes this species is known as eurabbie.

Southern blue gum is very similar to *E. globulus*, but is most easily distinguished by the fact that it has groups of three flowers, which are rather smaller than the solitary flowers of *E. globulus*. The name *bicostata* refers to the two ridges on the calyx of each bud; these are formed when the three buds are pressed closely together during their early development, and usually persist as faint ridges on the fruits. Flowers occur in winter.

Both the blue gums have rough, grey or brown bark at the base of the trunk. This is shed in long strips, leaving a rather shaggy appearance. The upper part of the trunk is smooth, usually a blue-grey colour.

Southern blue gum is also a very vigorous tree, and casts a very heavy shade. It is useful for parkland planting, where a dense stand is needed quickly, but because it suppresses most vegetation beneath it, and the bark, leaves and fruits are slow to decompose when they are shed, it is rather an untidy tree. It is not to be recommended for the home garden.

PLATE 131

MAIDEN'S GUM (*Eucalyptus maidenii*)

This species is named in honour of Joseph Henry

Maiden, who was Government Botanist of New South Wales from 1896 to 1924 and whose writings on the eucalypts are far more extensive than those of any other botanist. His *Critical Revision of the Genus Eucalyptus*, in eight volumes, covered all the species known at the time and included life-size drawings of leaves, buds and fruits. He was responsible for the naming and description of a great many species, and his works are still one of the most valuable references to the genus.

Maiden's gum is closely related to Tasmanian and southern blue gums (*E. globulus* and *E. bicostata*) and continues the series in being rather less coarse in its parts, with smaller buds and fruits, and these are borne in groups of seven, in contrast to the single buds of *E. globulus* and the groups of three for *E. bicostata*. Maiden's gum still has rather thick, leathery, glossy, green leaves, however, and specimens of intermediate leaves three feet long have been recorded. The mature leaves are usually four to six inches long. Flowering occurs during winter.

E. maidenii usually has only a short stocking of persistent, greyish bark at the base of the trunk, the upper bark being smooth, blotched, with a yellow or blue-grey tint.

Maiden's gum occurs on the south coast of New South Wales and in eastern Gippsland, where it grows on moist, rather heavy soils, usually on the lower slopes. It may reach 180 feet in height and is usually straight-boled. Its juvenile foliage of large, glaucous leaves, carried on four-winged stems, is conspicuous and attractive in the undergrowth.

PLATE 132

MOUNTAIN GREY GUM (*Eucalyptus cypellocarpa*)

This tree may grow to 200 feet in height, with a diameter of eight feet, so it must be regarded as one of the larger eucalypts. Usually, however, it is much smaller than this, and over much of its range rarely reaches 150 feet.

Mountain grey gum is most common in Victoria, from the Grampians to east Gippsland, but it also occurs on the coastal side of the southern tablelands of New South Wales, and there are isolated occurrences on the central and northern tablelands of that State.

The word *cypellocarpa* refers to the goblet shape of the capsules. These are carried in groups of seven, on short stalks; the buds are rather elongated, with a pointed operculum and are distinct from any of the related species.

Mountain grey gum occurs on a wide range of soils, and will tolerate frost and light snow. It is only moderately drought-hardy, however.

This tree is rather large for home gardens, but makes a very attractive specimen tree for park planting. The smooth bark is shed in large, irregular plates to leave a mottled yellow, grey and white surface. It has a moderately dense crown, with long, narrow leaves which are dark glossy green on both surfaces, and it flowers in midsummer.

PLATE 133

BOG GUM OR FLAT-ROOT (*Eucalyptus kitsoniana*)

This is a species which occurs on the poorer soils and wet sites in the Gippsland region of Victoria. It has also been collected from near Nelson, on the coast in far south-western Victoria. It is one of the relatively few mallees of the moister part of Australia, being apparently adapted to survive in wetter than normal conditions, rather than the dry conditions which are typical of the inland mallee country.

E. kitsoniana has the large underground root-stock or lignotuber which characterises the mallees, and from which numerous slender, smooth-barked stems arise. The large, ovate, opposite leaves which are usually present are intermediate type, the adult leaves being much smaller, lanceolate, and with a fine point.

This species was described in 1904 by J. G. Luehmann, curator of the National Herbarium, Melbourne, and named in honour of A. E. Kitson, a Victorian geologist. Luehmann's original name for this species was *E. kitsonii*, but it was found that this name had already been used for a fossil species, so J. H. Maiden, in 1916, republished the original description and changed the name to *E. kitsoniana*.

Bog gum is usually only three or four feet tall, but in a few localities it grows to tree form, reaching about twenty feet. It has a smooth, grey bark, with large, ovate, leathery intermediate leaves and smaller, but still leathery, adult leaves. The rounded, sessile buds are borne in close clusters of seven, and it flowers in midsummer.

PLATE 134

OMEO GUM (*Eucalyptus neglecta*)

This species was collected by A. W. Howitt from swampy flats near Omeo, in the Victorian highlands, at an elevation of about 3,000 feet, and was described and named by Maiden in 1904.

Growing in dense thickets, seldom more than twelve feet high, with a mass of dark green foliage, Omeo gum seems to be a very useful tree for windbreaks on alpine sites.

The bark at the base of older trees is slightly fibrous, but on the younger trees it is smooth and tends to be shed in long ribbons. The young stems are often square and covered by a bluish wax, as are the juvenile leaves. These are sessile, oval, thick and leathery, and often have a wavy margin.

The buds and fruits are carried in dense clusters in the axils of the leaves. The buds are small and ovoid while the fruits are nearly hemispheric, with a prominent disc and exserted valves. Flowers are seen in summer.

PLATE 135

YELLOW GUM (*Eucalyptus johnstonii*)

Growing to 200 feet on good sites, but small and stunted at high altitudes, *E. johnstonii* is rather variable, being locally frequent on the mountains of Tasmania's central plateau, and in the south and west of the island State. It occurs at altitudes of 2,000 to 4,500 feet, usually on badly drained sandstone.

The bark of this tree is shed in large scales or irregular sheets, leaving a short stocking of rough bark at the base, and smooth, orange, red or yellowish-green bark above. The adult leaves vary in shape from lanceolate and slightly curved, through ovate to orbicular, becoming generally broader at higher altitudes, but all rather leathery, glossy green and with a wavy margin.

The sessile buds are borne in umbels of three on short, strap-shaped stalks. The operculum is usually short, bluntly conic or flattened, with a central point, whilst the calyx tube is usually angular. The flowers occur in summer.

This species was originally called *E. muelleri*, but that name had already been used for a different species, so in 1924 Maiden gave it the present name, to honour Robert Mackenzie Johnston, a botanist who did considerable work on the Tasmanian flora during the latter half of the nineteenth century.

PLATE 136

CAMDEN WOOLLYBUTT (*Eucalyptus macarthurii*)

This species has a restricted natural occurrence in the south-eastern part of New South Wales, but has been planted as a street tree in other parts of southern Australia as well as in California. Camden woollybutt is normally found on deep, fertile clay loams, in a region of cool, moist climate, from the Blue Mountains, west of Sydney, to the southern tablelands south of Mittagong.

The common name commemorates the town of Camden, in the district where John Macarthur established the first flock of merino sheep in Australia. His son William collected botanical specimens during the middle part of the nineteenth century and it is in honour of Sir William Macarthur that the botanical name was given.

On good sites *E. macarthurii* may reach 130 feet in height and four feet in diameter but it is usually much smaller, and commonly less than fifty feet tall. Growing often in woodland formation, it still has a relatively straight trunk but carries branches from near ground level. This is an advantage as a farm tree or park specimen but may be a disadvantage for street planting, where clear access or visibility is needed. For this reason, and because planted trees have suffered both from dying back of branches and from wood-rot, in places such as Canberra, this species should be regarded as doubtful for street planting.

E. macarthurii leaves have been used for the distillation of geranyl acetate and geraniol, which are used in perfumery.

PLATE 137

GULLY GUM (*Eucalyptus smithii*)

In the southern tableland region of New South Wales, on fertile loams derived from basalt, *E. smithii* occurs as a rather large tree, with dark, often deeply furrowed bark on the lower part of the trunk, and smooth, brownish bark on the upper part and branches. The smooth bark is shed annually in long strips, which often hang from the branch forks.

Gully gum has a dense crown of glossy, dark green leaves, which are long and narrow, and hang vertically. The small, cream flowers are borne in umbels of seven, and are followed by medium-sized, hemispherical or ovoid fruits with exserted valves. It flowers in late summer.

E. smithii is one of the species which are used for the distillation of oil. It was described and named by R. T. Baker in honour of his colleague, H. G. Smith, with whom he produced the book *A Research on the Eucalypts Especially in Regard to Their Essential Oils.*

PLATE 138

MANNA GUM (*Eucalyptus viminalis*)

E. viminalis was discovered by J. J. Labillardière, who sailed from France in 1799, with D'Entrecasteau, on a voyage in search of La Perouse. This expedition landed near the southern tip of Tasmania, and the first specimen of manna gum is assumed to have been collected from the vicinity of Recherche Bay. This is the most southerly occurrence of a species which is found over a wide area, from the Mt Lofty Range of South Australia, across Victoria, and along the New South Wales tablelands to the Queensland border.

Known also as ribbon gum and white gum, this species is a very attractive tree. Usually smooth-barked over most of its tall, straight trunk and branches, with a stocking of rough bark at the base and often with ribbons of dead bark hanging from the branch forks, it is also found with rough bark extending over much of the trunk. Flowers occur over much of the year.

Manna gum is common on cool, moist sites, especially in eastern Victoria and eastern Tasmania. In Victoria it is the most common food for koalas, although these animals also eat the leaves of many other species.

The word *viminalis* refers to the twiggy nature of the crown, with long, slender branchlets carrying pendant leaves which are light green, long and narrow. They have rather prominent venation, and copious oil glands which exude a sticky oil when the leaf is broken.

Manna gum is one of the most cold-hardy species, and combined with its rapid growth, attractive form and pink or pale yellow to white wood, this makes it a popular tree for ornamental and commercial planting.

PLATE 139

ROUGH-BARKED MANNA GUM (*Eucalyptus huberana*)

In the regions of higher rainfall in South Australia, from the Mt Lofty Range southwards, and in southern Victoria, there are trees which are obviously closely related to the manna gum (*E. viminalis*), but have rough, grey, more or less fibrous bark on the trunk and to varying heights on the branches. These trees also produce buds and fruits in groups of five to seven, as well as in threes, as is typical of the southern forms of manna gum. These trees have been identified with the name *E. huberana*, given originally by the French botanist Naudin to a single tree grown by M. Huber at Nice in France. Other botanists have considered that they are forms of manna gum, or constitute a separate variety of that species. The name *E. huberana* has also been applied to trees with similar characteristics growing in Tasmania and northern New South Wales.

More recently, however, a separate species with rough bark and seven-flowered umbels has been recognised in western Victoria and named scent-bark (*E. aromaphloia*) and it was considered that many of the trees called *E. huberana* were actually of hybrid origin between *E. viminalis* and *E. aromaphloia* in South Australia and western Victoria, and between *E. viminalis* and other rough-barked trees in other regions.

PLATE 140

ARGYLE APPLE (*Eucalyptus cinerea*)

Occurring commonly along watercourses or on flat to gently undulating country, and usually on infertile, sandy or shaly soils, Argyle apple has a discontinuous distribution from Bathurst in the central part of New South Wales's western slopes, through the southern tablelands to eastern Victoria. It is sometimes known as mealy stringybark.

It is an attractive tree with a short bole covered by reddish-brown, fibrous bark which extends to the smaller branches. The crown is compact and dense, casting a low, heavy shade, so that this is a good shelter tree. Under natural conditions the intermediate leaves are maintained over the whole or greater part of the crown. These are opposite, sessile, ovate and blue-grey. The tree usually flowers in this condition, the three-flowered umbels being borne in the axils of the upper leaves, and covered by a white, waxy coating. The cream to yellow flowers appear in early summer.

Under cultivation, *E. cinerea* frequently produces adult foliage, as in the painting, giving the tree a different and usually even more attractive appearance. The branchlets become longer and often droop, and the longer, lanceolate leaves are silvery white. The botanical name *cinerea* means 'ash-coloured', referring to the white coating on the leaves, buds and fruits.

Argyle apple is normally slow-growing, but under cultivation can reach eight feet in three years. As it is only a small tree, its serves a very useful role as an ornamental. It is moderately hardy to frost and drought.

PLATE 141

BLUE MALLEE (*Eucalyptus gamophylla*)

The name *gamophylla* means 'joined leaves', a reference to the feature of this species where the bases of the opposite leaves are joined across the stem. This is typical of the species, although not invariable. It occurs in deep, red sands, including sand dunes, in central Australia and in adjacent parts of South Australia and Western Australia. Though referred to in several publications as the twin-leaved gum, it is more popularly known as blue mallee in pastoral areas of central Australia.

Blue mallee is invariably a many-stemmed mallee, with some fibrous or flaky bark peeling off below, and with grey or pale pink, smooth bark above. It grows from ten to twenty-five feet high, and its leaves are markedly glaucous or blue-grey.

Drought- and frost-resistant, the blue mallee is quick-growing, would make an attractive garden shrub and is ideal for windbreaks in dry, sandy soil. It flowers in May and June.

Very few *Eucalyptus* species are grazed by animals, but in drought times in central Australia this species is heavily grazed by cattle.

PLATE 142

GUM-BARKED COOLIBAH (*Eucalyptus intertexta*)

Growing in western New South Wales, northern South Australia, southern parts of the Northern Territory, and in the Cavanagh Range of Western Australia, this species has also proved useful cultivated in arid parts of some Mediterranean countries. It grows to eighty feet high, but is more often forty to sixty feet tall, with rough, grey bark to about ten feet on the trunk and smooth to grey-white on the branches. At times it is mallee-like on rocky hills.

The name *intertexta* means 'interwoven', a reference to the tough fibres of the hard timber which, however, is not markedly durable. The species is also known as coolibah, but it is different from the species more properly known as coolibah (*E. microtheca*); the fruits of the gum-barked coolibah are about twice as big as those of the coolibah, and they curve slightly inwards at the top.

E. intertexta grows in low-lying, open plains, sometimes near areas where seasonal surface water may be evident. It can also grow close to saltpans and is reasonably salt-tolerant. It provides good shade, and is suitable for avenue planting, or for use as firewood.

Flowering can be intermittent, but mainly between April and August. The trees are notably drought- and frost-resistant.

PLATE 143

GYMPIE MESSMATE (*Eucalyptus cloeziana*)

Although it occurs over a very wide area in eastern Queensland, *E. cloeziana* is common only in disconnected locations. The best development is in the Gympie district, at altitudes of 200 to 1,200 feet, but it is also found at about 3,000 feet on the Atherton Tableland.

Gympie messmate occurs in a mixture with other eucalypts, on moist sites, and occasionally on the margins of rain-forests. It has the unusual feature amongst eucalypts of being able to tolerate considerable shade when young, and because it sheds its lower branches rapidly, is able to grow to a tall, clean-boled tree. The bark of the trunk and larger branches is persistent, soft and flaky-fibrous, and the leaves are dark, glossy green on the upper surface and paler below, forming a rather dense crown.

The flowers of this species are also unusual, being borne in compound inflorescences (panicles) on leafless, lower parts of the twigs in March and April. The small, cream flowers are followed by hemispheric or almost globular fruits.

The name 'messmate' has been applied to several eucalypts and usually means that these are companion trees to other species. Gympie messmate often occurs in pure stands, however, particularly on the more favourable sites.

PLATE 144

SOAP MALLEE (*Eucalyptus diversifolia*)

Sometimes this species is called white mallee or coastal mallee in South Australia, where it grows along the southern coastal area extending westward into the Nullarbor Plain area in Western Australia, and it is also on Goat Island and Kangaroo Island.

E. diversifolia is generally a mallee from ten to twenty feet high with smooth, grey, white, or light brown bark which becomes deciduous in long strips; it can also be a small tree. It grows in sandy or calcareous soil which is often shallow. Flowering time is from November to January, but this period is usually extended in cultivation.

Though not an outstanding species, the soap mallee can be a useful garden shrub, and it is an excellent windbreak species. It prefers about sixteen inches of rain annually, but some forms should grow adequately in drier climates.

The name *diversifolia*, meaning 'different leaves', was applied by A. J. A. Bonpland, a French botanist and explorer, and he was referring to the fact that the juvenile leaves differed from the adult ones. However, this is a feature of all eucalypts, not specifically of the soap mallee.

PLATE 145

SWAN RIVER BLACKBUTT (*Eucalyptus patens*)

One of the many species called blackbutt, this eucalypt has rough, fibrous, dark grey bark on the trunk and branches, and this becomes blackened by bushfires. The tree can grow up to 150 feet, but is more usually from eighty to one hundred feet high with a bole which is about half of the total height, and which can be from three to five feet in diameter. Swan River blackbutt inhabits the moister parts of the jarrah (*E. marginata*) and karri (*E. diversicolor*) forest in the south-west of Western Australia, and in these favoured places it forms small, almost pure stands. The soil is mostly dark loam on top of clay.

Leaves which are narrower and paler bluish-green help to distinguish this blackbutt from jarrah, which it sometimes resembles. It also has smaller fruits with a narrower rim. The name *patens* means 'standing open', and this may refer to the open spreading habit of the tree.

The timber is very tough and durable, being suitable for flooring, panelling, sleepers or packing cases. Its quality is comparable to jarrah, but it is not as plentiful. In a plantation in South Africa, *E. patens* grew to 103 feet in thirty-five years.

Flowers occur from November to February.

PLATE 146

WEEPING GUM (*Eucalyptus sepulcralis*)

Baron Ferdinand von Mueller, the Victorian botanist who named this plant *sepulcralis*, intended it as a reference to the weeping habit as reminiscent of cemeteries in Europe. It is a small tree, about eighteen to twenty feet high, with flowers, leaves, fruits and even the branches pendulous, so that the weeping habit is most evident. The stems are thin, white and smooth, sometimes greyish-brown at the base. The large, urn-shaped fruit is distinctive.

Weeping gum occurs only in small areas in a small semi-circle southwards from Ravensthorpe in Western Australia, usually in sandy soil on rocky hills.

Flowering is in summer from January to March. Weeping gum is a most attractive, small, ornamental tree, but it needs protection from winds in order to develop a good shape. It is moderately frost- and drought-resistant.

PLATE 147

JARRAH (*Eucalyptus marginata*)

A timber which is famed throughout the world for its toughness and durability, jarrah is suitable for many purposes including piles, sleepers, furniture, flooring, or in past days, paving blocks. It is easily worked, and is resistant to termites.

Jarrah grows as a tree up to 135 feet, but is mostly up to about one hundred feet high with a straight bole about half of the total height, and about three to six feet in diameter. It has red-grey, fibrous bark. The name *marginata* refers to a thickened margin of the leaves, and this can help in identification.

The Darling Range in Western Australia shows the best development of jarrah on low hills usually in lateritic gravel on top of clay. However, the species extends in a belt twenty or thirty miles wide from Gin Gin, north of Perth, southwards to Albany.

Attempts to cultivate plantations of jarrah overseas have not been successful. In its native area, too, some stands are being attacked by a fungal infection and research is being carried out in order to overcome this threat to the timber industry of Western Australia.

Flowering times are irregular but mainly between September and February.

PLATE 148

YELLOW TINGLE (*Eucalyptus guilfoylei*)

William Robert Guilfoyle, a former Director of the Melbourne Botanic Gardens, is honoured by the naming of this species. The term 'tingle' is an abbreviation of 'tingle tingle', apparently a native name.

Yellow tingle grows in low-lying areas or in deep gullies where there is rich, loamy soil in a small area between Denmark and the Shannon River, on the south coast of Western Australia. The rainfall in this region is about fifty inches annually. The trees grow from eighty to 150 feet high, with a bole of about fifty feet and a diameter of about four feet. Dark grey, fibrous or stringy bark covers the trunk and branches.

The timber is yellow and is hard, durable and termite-resistant, but is not as economically important as jarrah (*E. marginata*) because of its limited occurrence. Club-shaped buds and pear-shaped fruits in clusters up to seven or eight on long, common stalks are distinctive features.

Except for a group of trees in South Africa, yellow tingle has not succeeded in overseas plantings.

Flowers occur from December to February.

PLATE 149

BLACKBUTT (*Eucalyptus pilularis*)

From Fraser Island in south-eastern Queensland to the south coast of New South Wales, blackbutt is a conspicuous part of the sclerophyllous forest. It is also the most important tree for timber production and is regarded as the 'bread and butter' tree of the forest services.

Blackbutt is a moderate to large tree, reaching over 200 feet in height, with diameters up to seven feet. The trunk is straight and half to two-thirds of the total height, with a rather open crown and an erect, branching habit. It often forms pure stands on well-drained sites, usually with sandy loams, but is occasionally found on heavier soils.

Growing in a region of equable climate with mild summers, cool winters and only occasional frosts, and with an annual rainfall of thirty-five to sixty inches distributed uniformly or with a summer maximum, blackbutt is not especially hardy, but is a fast-growing tree, rivalling the rose gum (*E. grandis*) on suitable sites.

Under cultivation outside Australia, it has not been very successful, the few reports of its establishment being followed by early death or stagnation, suggesting that more attention should be given to its root development.

The name *pilularis* refers to the globular or hemispheric fruits, whilst 'blackbutt' is an allusion to the fact that the rough, finely fibrous bark on the lower part of the trunk is usually blackened by the fires which occur so frequently in this type of forest. The bark on the upper trunk and branches is smooth and white or yellowish. Flowers appear in summer.

PLATE 150

YELLOW STRINGYBARK (*Eucalyptus muellerana*)

This is a tree which is called a stringybark, although the bark is often more compact and less fibrous than other stringybarks. It is brown on the surface, but the inner bark is yellow, and this, with the yellow-brown colour of the wood, is responsible for the common name.

The botanical name honours Ferdinand von Mueller, one of the outstanding botanists in Australia's history.

This tree provides a most valuable timber which is strong, durable, straight-grained and has been widely used, particularly in Victoria, for posts and piles. It has a reputation for durability in salt water, and has been used for harbour works as well as general building.

Yellow stringybark reaches its best development in the Gippsland region of Victoria, where trees of 150 feet in height have been recorded. It also occurs in south-eastern New South Wales and in the Mt Lofty Range in South Australia. A tall, straight tree with a rather dense crown of glossy, green leaves, it is quite an attractive tree in the forest. The multi-flowered umbels, with conic opercula on the buds show its relationship to the blackbutt (*E. pilularis*) as do the hemispheric or sub-globular fruits with their flat discs and short valves. Flowering is mainly in summer.

E. muellerana grows on moderately fertile, sheltered sites in hilly country.

PLATE 151

WHITE MAHOGANY (*Eucalyptus umbra*)

There are three species of eucalypts which are commonly called white mahogany, *E. acmenioides*, *E. umbra* and *E. carnea*. The last-mentioned is sometimes regarded as a subspecies of *E. umbra*, but is distinct in its natural occurrence. 'Mahogany' is used generally for trees which have rough, fibrous bark, similar to the stringybarks, and the term 'white' refers to the white or pale brown wood, to distinguish these species from the red mahoganies.

While *E. umbra* may reach eighty feet in height, it is usually much smaller than this, and frequently grows to only about twenty feet, where it occurs on the edges of coastal swamps in Queensland. It seems to be able to tolerate a wide range of rather poor conditions, from tight, badly drained clays to shallow sands over rock, and occurs from near Sydney to the central Queensland coast.

White mahogany is not a very attractive tree, having a rough, fibrous, light brown bark and a dense crown of thick, dark green leaves. It flowers in spring. The botanical name, meaning 'shading', refers to the dense shade it casts, although on dry sites this is not so marked.

PLATE 152

TALLOW-WOOD (*Eucalyptus microcorys*)

Tallow-wood is a tree which grows to a moderate height but sometimes reaches very large dimensions, a tree 230 feet tall being recorded in Queensland. It is a distinctive tree, especially in its younger stages, with a brown bark, horizontal branching habit and attractive, light green foliage, with flowers from winter to early summer.

The bark is softly fibrous, with thin layers of cork appearing as small, smooth or flaky patches. The timber of this species is yellowish-brown and is very strong and durable; the name tallow-wood refers to the greasy texture of the polished wood, which makes a fine dance floor.

Tallow-wood grows over a relatively small area from near Newcastle in New South Wales to near Maryborough in Queensland. In this area it occurs from near sea level to about 2,500 feet, and, while it grows best on deep loams, it also occurs on clays and sandy soils.

This is another of the few species of eucalypt which will tolerate shading when young. Tallow-wood has soft, thin, pale green leaves which contrast with the usual leathery texture of 'gum leaves' and it carries its flowers in compound inflorescences at the ends of the branchlets, so that, in flower, it is even more conspicuous in the forest.

The name *microcorys* refers to the tiny cap, or operculum, of the bud. The long, club-shaped buds and long, conic fruits, which are usually pale brown or yellowish when mature, are also distinct among the eucalypts.

PLATE 153

WHITE STRINGYBARK (*Eucalyptus eugenioides*)

The stringybarks comprise a number of groups of closely related species, with many intermediate forms, so that the task of classifying them is very difficult. All have brown or grey-brown, coarsely fibrous bark, which can be pulled off in long strips.

The major division of the stringybarks is based on the colour of the wood, so that we have red, white and brown stringybarks. Within each of these groups there are several species, and opinions differ amongst botanists as to how many species there are. The white stringybarks are common on rather poor soils along the coast from Gippsland in Victoria to south-eastern Queensland. They have distinctive juvenile leaves which are often undulate and covered by tufts of hair. The adult leaves usually are oblique with a shiny surface, whilst the buds are borne in large clusters, usually with very short pedicels.

Typically, the white stringybarks have globular or hemispheric fruits, with a rounded, reddish disc and small valves. Because of the very short stalks, these fruits are tightly clustered and often become slightly compressed at the base.

Eugenia is a genus related to *Eucalyptus*, and has dark green, glossy leaves. The epithet *eugenioides* was used by the Austrian botanist, Wilhelm Sieber, when he described this species as resembling a *Eugenia*.

This species flowers in spring to early summer.

PLATE 154

RED STRINGYBARK (*Eucalyptus macrorhyncha*)

As the name implies, red stringybark has red or red-brown wood, in contrast to the white and brown stringybarks. Also in contrast to those groups, red stringybark occurs principally in inland, rather dry areas. It is common on the foothills of the Dividing Range, particularly on the inland side, of Victoria and New South Wales, but also occurs in the Gippsland region of Victoria.

The botanical name *macrorhyncha* means 'large-beaked', and refers to the long, conic or beaked operculum on each bud. On a closely related species, Cannon's stringybark (*E. cannonii*), the buds are angular as well.

Red stringybark is mainly a tree of the dry forests which occur on rocky hills at intermediate altitudes, but it is also found in woodland formation, where as a short-boled tree with a dense, rounded crown, it presents a distinctive appearance. This species can grow on dry sites in regions where high summer temperatures contrast with heavy winter frosts and occasional snow. It can grow to over one hundred feet in height, but is commonly much less than this. It is a good shade tree for farmlands although it has a tendency to die back in droughts.

Flowering occurs during late summer.

PLATE 155

BROWN STRINGYBARK (*Eucalyptus baxteri*)

In 1790, J. E. Smith described a eucalypt from specimens growing near Sydney and named it *E. capitellata*. This is evidently the small stringybark with large fruits which grows in that district. Later the name was extended to cover trees in Victoria, South Australia and on the Blue Mountains in New South Wales, but these have since been described as distinct species, *E. baxteri* and *E. blaxlandii*.

E. baxteri is common in western Victoria, especially in the Grampians, and in the rolling country in the south-west of that State. It also occurs across the border in South Australia, extending as far west as Kangaroo Island. To the east, it is found in the southern foothills of the Dividing Range and in east Gippsland.

This is a typical stringybark, with brown, fibrous bark persistent to the small branches, thick, glossy leaves which are oblique at the base, and hemispheric or globular fruits with a wide, convex disc and short valves. Flowers occur in late summer.

Brown stringybark will grow on rather infertile, sandy soils, but on such sites rarely reaches fifty feet in height. On deeper, more fertile soils, particularly in the moister areas, it grows to about one hundred feet, with a coarsely branched, rather dense crown.

PLATE 156

GRAMPIANS GUM (*Eucalyptus alpina*)

This stunted tree, with its broad, shiny leaves, was discovered by the Mitchell expedition of 1836, and formally described and named by John Lindley, who was professor of botany at University College in London in 1838. It is a low, spreading tree which occurs naturally along the highest parts of the Grampians in central western Victoria. In this rather harsh environment, the species has developed a resistance to the winter winds, which makes it valuable for shelter belts at lower altitudes.

E. alpina has a stringy bark, and other features such as the thick, leathery, ovate leaves which are asymmetrical and have a tiny point at the tip, also suggest a relationship with the brown stringybark (*E. baxteri*). The buds and fruits are quite distinct, however. The buds are borne in sessile clusters of three to five, often on leafless lengths of twig, and flowers occur in summer to early winter. The buds are extremely warty and irregular so that it would be difficult to recognise

a formal shape such as is usual amongst eucalypts. The fruits are rather large and woody, closely pressed to the stem, and roughly hemispheric, but with a narrow disc and large, exserted valves.

PLATE 157

BLUE-LEAVED STRINGYBARK (*Eucalyptus agglomerata*)

Occurring on the lower parts of the New South Wales central and southern tablelands, and on the adjacent coastal country, *E. agglomerata* is distinctive for the blue-green colour of the leaves. This may be quite conspicuous, and where the topography is steep, altitudinal zoning causes a distinct band of blue to appear across the hillside, in contrast to the neighbouring greens.

Blue-leaved stringybark is a typical stringybark, with rough, fibrous bark, hairy juvenile leaves, multi-flowered umbels and rather small fruits which are sessile, hemispheric or globular, and borne in tight clusters. This is the origin of the botanical name.

This is a species which produces a useful timber. It is largely used for local building material and has a reputation for durability. It occurs on sedimentary rocks, frequently on rather shallow soils of low fertility. Flowering is in early winter.

PLATE 158

MESSMATE STRINGYBARK (*Eucalyptus obliqua*)

Historically, this is a most important eucalypt, as it was the first species botanically described in literature, being so described in 1789 by the French magistrate and botanist, L'Héritier, from a specimen collected in 1777 by William Anderson and David Nelson on Bruny Island off the east coast of Tasmania.

It is not a typical stringybark, being more closely related to the ashes, and particularly to alpine ash (*E. delegatensis*). It has brown, fibrous bark extending to the small branches, and large, glossy, green leaves. The name *obliqua* refers to the oblique base of the mature leaf, and the intermediate leaves are also oblique, but this is characteristic of the whole ash group. Another leaf character which is shared by the ashes is the acute angle which the rather prominent secondary veins make with the midrib. Messmate stringybark differs from alpine ash in having dark green intermediate leaves; alpine ash has glaucous intermediate leaves and the upper part of the trunk and branches are smooth.

E. obliqua is one of the most valuable timber-producing trees of Victoria and Tasmania, but occurs also in South Australia and on Kangaroo Island, whilst in New South Wales it extends to the northern tablelands where it grows to altitudes of 4,000 feet. In Tasmania the upper level of occurrence is less than 2,000 feet. It is a species of the relatively poorer sites in moist, cool climates, and will stand snow and frost; at its best it is a very large tree, specimens of 225 feet having been recorded. In the drier parts of its range it is a very much smaller tree, however.

Flowering occurs in summer.

PLATE 159

BROWN BARREL (*Eucalyptus fastigata*)

Brown barrel is usually a moderately large tree, reaching 150 feet in height and six feet in diameter, with a long, straight bole and a relatively large, well-branched crown.

The bark persists on the trunk and large branches as a grey-brown, finely fibrous covering, but is shed from the branches to leave a smooth, white surface. The rather small, curved leaves are glossy, dark green, with acute venation which shows the relation of this species to the ashes. Typical of the ashes, too, are the many-flowered umbels of pointed buds, but brown barrel, like mountain ash (*E. regnans*) bears pairs of umbels in each leaf axil, while the other species have single umbels. The fruits are pear-shaped or conic, tapering into the stalk, and with a moderately wide, domed disc and usually three valves.

Brown barrel is abundant only in small areas from the northern tablelands of New South Wales to the far eastern part of Victoria. It is a species of good soils in cool, moist climates and appears not to be very adaptable in its natural area, yet in New Zealand it has been widely planted and has proved to be one of the most useful species.

It will tolerate frosts down to about twelve degrees F, and flowers in summer.

In the original description of this species, Deane and Maiden 'propose the name *fastigata* for it, in allusion to the shape of the operculum and leaves'. The allusion is not clear, as *fastigatus* means exalted, whilst *fastigium* means summit, slope or gable.

PLATE 160

MOUNTAIN ASH (*Eucalyptus regnans*)

The tallest species of *Eucalyptus*, and the tallest hardwood in the world, although surpassed by some of the north American conifers, *E. regnans* reigns above the lesser species in the deep, friable soils and moist climates of Victoria and Tasmania. Trees well over 300 feet tall have been measured, but the tallest tree known to be standing at present is 322 feet. The name *regnans* means 'ruling or 'reigning', a reference to the height.

Mountain ash does not reach diameters as great as some of the other species, however; typical measurements are between six and ten feet. The tree usually has a very long, straight trunk with a crown which looks disproportionately small and is rather open. The trunk has a stocking of rough, sub-fibrous bark up to fifty feet, the remainder being shed in long ribbons to leave a smooth, white or greenish-grey surface. Flowers occur in summer.

In Victoria, mountain ash is restricted mainly to the mountains in the eastern half of the State, with a small occurrence in the Otway Ranges, to the south-west of Melbourne. The Tasmanian occurrence is mainly in the Huon and Derwent valleys, in the south-east, and in the north-west, at altitudes below about 2,000 feet, although it occurs up to 3,000 feet on the mainland.

Mountain ash is one of the most important hardwoods of Australia, being widely used for interior and building construction as well as being the most important eucalypt used in the Australian wood-pulp industry.

PLATE 161

ALPINE ASH (*Eucalyptus delegatensis*)

Growing to a large size, and producing valuable timber, alpine ash is one of the important commercial species of south-eastern Australia. It is relatively limited in distribution, in the Australian Capital Territory and southwards into Victoria, where it occurs at altitudes of 3,000 to 4,500 feet. It also occurs extensively in Tasmania at altitudes of between 1,000 and 3,000 feet.

Alpine ash, as its name implies, is a mountain species, occurring on deep, moist soils, especially those of the upper slopes, and on the mainland it favours the southern and eastern aspects.

This tree was named *E. gigantea* by Hooker, but it was realised later that this name had already been used for the Western Australian giant, karri, so alpine ash was renamed *E. delegatensis* by R. T. Baker, to indicate that it was found in the vicinity of Delegate in southern New South Wales.

It grows to over 200 feet, with stem diameters of up to seven feet, a long, straight bole covered by brown, fibrous bark, and smooth, white, cream or blue-grey branches. The adult leaves are long and curved, and dull green on both surfaces, whilst the juvenile leaves are large, ovate and silvery grey.

The fruits of this species are very similar to those of the closely related messmate stringybark (*E. obliqua*), being rather large and woody, barrel-shaped with a flat top, or pear-shaped.

Alpine ash is very frost-resistant, coming from regions where snow is common and frosts are likely to occur at any time during the year. Flowers appear in late summer.

PLATE 162

SILVERTOP ASH (*Eucalyptus sieberi*)

Known also as coast ash and, in Tasmania, as iron-bark, silvertop ash grows in rather warmer localities than the other members of this group. It is common in eastern Victoria, between the Dividing Range and the sea, and extends along the coast of New South Wales as far north as the Hawkesbury River, extending inland in the Blue Mountain region to near Blackheath, at an altitude of about 3,500 feet. In Tasmania it occurs in a small strip along the eastern coast.

Silvertop ash is a species which grows on sandy soils which may be very low in nutrients and often shallow. It will stand light frost, but is usually found on relatively warm situations, such as the ridges in hilly country, where the cold air drains away into the valleys.

This species was named after Wilhelm Sieber, a Viennese botanist who collected plants in Australia in 1823.

It is a distinctive species with a thick, dark brown and deeply furrowed bark on the trunk and main branches, but smooth, white or yellowish bark on the smaller branches. The young plants have silver-grey leaves which are held on edge, extending out from the stem, and the young leaves are bright red. Saplings have brown, flaky-fibrous bark on the lower trunk, and smooth, white or waxy bark above, so that they have little resemblance to the older trees. The flowering time is in early summer.

PLATE 163

YERTCHUK (*Eucalyptus consideniana*)

This tree is common on sandy, infertile soils in eastern Victoria and the south coast of New South Wales, and it flowers in early summer.

Although it is a member of the ash group, yertchuk looks more like a peppermint to the casual observer. It has rough, closely fibrous, grey bark on the trunk and large branches, the smaller branches being smooth and white. The rough bark is prickly to the touch, and this feature has led to the name 'prickly-barked stringybark' in parts of Victoria.

The leaves are lanceolate and curved, being dull green on both surfaces, and moderately thick. Growing on infertile sites, *E. consideniana* rarely reaches a large size and is not a very picturesque tree. The timber is regarded as of low quality but this is one of the trees used for the production of paper pulp.

The common name is apparently of aboriginal origin. The botanical name commemorates First-assistant Surgeon D. Considen who came to Australia with the first fleet in 1788 and was considered by Maiden to be 'the founder of the eucalyptus oil industry'.

PLATE 164

BASTARD TALLOW-WOOD (*Eucalyptus planchoniana*)

Occurring on infertile, sandy soils on the north coast of New South Wales and south-eastern coastal Queensland, *E. planchoniana* is known by various common names, such as needlebark and porcupine stringybark. More usually it is called bastard tallow-wood, the name giving an indication both of the timber and general appearance of the tree. The resemblance to tallow-wood (*E. microcorys*) is very much a superficial one, however. Although the barks of the two trees are brown and rather fibrous, and are distinctive amongst the gums, which more usually have grey barks, the crown of *E. planchoniana* is very dense and made up of large, thick, grey-green leaves.

Perhaps the most distinctive feature of this species is the large, barrel-shaped or ovoid fruits with conspicuous longitudinal ridges. The disc and valves are enclosed within the mouth of the fruit. The buds are also large and angular or ribbed, with a long, conic operculum and a tapering calyx tube. Flowers are seen in midsummer, and are a valuable source of honey.

This species was named by Ferdinand von Mueller in 1878 in honour of Dr J. E. Planchon, Director of the Botanic Garden at Montpellier in France and who was responsible for the introduction of many eucalypts into that country.

PLATE 165

YELLOW-TOPPED MALLEE ASH (*Eucalyptus luehmanniana*)

E. luehmanniana is one of a group of closely related species which occur on the sandstone country within one hundred miles of Sydney. These species all occur on shallow soils which are very low in fertility and often subject to periodic waterlogging and drying. They have developed the mallee habit, with large rootstocks and several stems and, because they appear to be closely related to the ash group, are known as mallee ashes.

E. luehmanniana was named by Ferdinand von Mueller in 1878, but he also at various times called it a variety of each of three other species in the group. J. G. Luehmann was von Mueller's assistant and later curator of the Melbourne Herbarium.

This species is distinguished chiefly by its broad juvenile leaves. It has yellow twigs which give rise to the common name, but this feature is also seen in others in the same group. Yellow-topped mallee ash occurs in cold, damp sites on the Hawkesbury sandstone between Helensburgh, south of Sydney, and Gosford, north of Sydney, and it flowers in spring.

The fruit of the yellow-topped mallee ash is represented on the current Australian five dollar note.

PLATE 166

PORT JACKSON MALLEE (*Eucalyptus obtusiflora*)

E. obtusiflora is one of several closely related species which are difficult to distinguish. As its name implies, the flower buds have obtuse opercula; they are club-shaped and borne in umbels of seven, on flattened stalks.

This species and the other mallee ashes occur on very poor soils in the central coast and tableland regions of New South Wales. They are found close to sea level on the shallow soils over sandstone, such as occur north and south of Sydney, and extend to about 3,000 feet in the Blue Mountains region. *E. obtusiflora* rarely grows to more than ten feet in height, and is commonly only four or five feet high. It has several stems about one inch in diameter, with shiny, green leaves held in an upright attitude, and it flowers in late winter.

As with other mallees, this species is very resistant to fire, and although the localities where it grows are often swept by bushfires, the plants survive through their underground lignotubers, from which new shoots quickly sprout.

PLATE 167

BLUE MOUNTAIN MALLEE ASH (*Eucalyptus stricta*)

E. stricta is common on the Blue Mountains, west of Sydney, but is also found further south, near Moss Vale and nearer to the coast, on the sandstone plateaux on each side of the Shoalhaven River. It is also recorded from Bega and one locality in Victoria. It is usually a many-stemmed mallee, but occasionally becomes a tree, and the specific name *stricta* appears to refer to the fact that it is often erect, as a tree, rarely reaching forty feet.

The Blue Mountain mallee ash is a hardy species, occurring at altitudes from 1,600 to 4,000 feet, with smooth bark which is shed in long strips, leaving a cream or grey-blotched surface. The leaves are narrow, shining, and rather thick, and the fruits are usually slightly constricted just below the opening.

This species usually flowers in January, but some flowers may be found in autumn or occasionally in winter. It appears to hybridise with several other species in the Blue Mountains.

PLATE 168

SNOW GUM (*Eucalyptus pauciflora*)

One of the best known, as well as one of the most widely distributed eucalypts, *E. pauciflora* seems to be also one of the most inappropriately named. The botanical name, given by Sieber, means 'few-flowered', yet it is a common sight to see trees covered with blossom during summer.

This species is also known as white sally, cabbage gum and weeping gum. It is typically a cold-country species, and one form, which is sometimes regarded as a variety and sometimes as a separate species, with the name *E. niphophila* (meaning 'snow-loving'), is the tree found at the tree-line of the mountains in the south-eastern part of the mainland of Australia. *E. pauciflora* is also found on the edges of frosty, treeless valleys in the mountains, and to near sea level in western Victoria and adjacent parts of South Australia. It is common in Tasmania, although here its high-altitude position is taken by other species.

Snow gum presents a remarkably attractive picture in the snow, with its short, curved trunk and smooth, blotched, yellow and white bark, often with patches of green or bronze. The bark is marked by insect scribbles, which help to distinguish it from mountain gum (*E. dalrympleana*) where they occur together. Snow gum has large, grey, leathery juvenile leaves with semi-parallel veins. The twigs are often bright red or yellow, although in the alpine form they are covered by a waxy bloom.

PLATE 169

BLACK SALLEE (*Eucalyptus stellulata*)

A small to medium-sized tree occurring on cold, wet sites throughout the higher parts of the Dividing Range in New South Wales and Victoria, black sallee appears to be one of the most cold-resistant eucalypts on the Australian mainland, but evidently will not tolerate drought as well as snow gum (*E. pauciflora*). These two species often occur close together, but usually in distinct zones, with black sallee on the wetter sites. In the higher parts of the mountains the treeless valleys which have wet heath or *Sphagnum* moss in the central part, are fringed by *E. stellulata* and *E. pauciflora*.

As its common name implies, the bark of older trees of this species is black or very dark, especially on the lower part where it is persistant as a hard, closely cracked surface. The upper part is olive green or slate-coloured, whilst the leaves are small, lanceolate and dark glossy green.

The botanical name means 'little stars' and refers to the clusters of pointed buds.

Black sallee will grow on a wide range of soils, from light sands derived from granite, to black, granular clays on basalt. It is an unusual tree, and well deserving of cultivation, particularly in cold, wet areas. It flowers from winter to spring, and sometimes into summer.

PLATE 170

LITTLE SALLY (*Eucalyptus moorei*)

Little sally is closely related to black sallee (*E. stellulata*), differing mainly in having narrow juvenile leaves and smaller mature leaves. It is often a mallee, whereas black sallee is normally a single-stemmed tree.

E. moorei was described by Maiden and Cambage in 1905, the specific name honouring C. Moore, who was New South Wales Government Botanist from 1848 to 1896.

This species is common on the Blue Mountains of central New South Wales and extends southwards along the tablelands to near Nimmitabel. It is often found in damp situations, such as the sources of streams, in the colder localities of the New South Wales mountains, at altitudes of 1,500 to 3,500 feet. Flowering in late summer or autumn, *E. moorei* appears to hybridise readily with several species of *Eucalyptus* and some of the hybrids have been given specific names.

Little sally has been recorded as growing to forty feet in height, but more often it is less than ten feet tall, forming thickets on the exposed sandstone plateaux where the soils are shallow and extremely low in nutrients.

PLATE 171

WHITE PEPPERMINT (*Eucalyptus linearis*)

This is a distinctive species with a smooth, white bark above a short, more or less scaly stocking, and a very light crown of linear leaves.

It is native to Tasmania, where it occurs only in the south-eastern region, flowering in the latter part of summer, but has been cultivated extensively, and the original description was made by the German botanist, F. Dehnhardt, in 1829, from specimens cultivated at Naples.

White peppermint thrives in cool, moist climates, and will tolerate frost and snow. It normally grows on rather poor soils but is rarely a large tree. The very narrow leaves to which the name *linearis* refers, and which have a strong peppermint smell when crushed, are almost sufficient to identify this species without anything else, but the many-flowered umbels of small, club-shaped buds and the rather small, flat-topped, conic to pear-shaped fruits also indicate that it is one of the peppermint group, in spite of its smooth bark.

E. linearis is a tree which is worthy of cultivation in cool, moist climates.

PLATE 172

RIVER PEPPERMINT (*Eucalyptus elata*)

This species has probably had more botanical names applied to it than any other eucalypt. Certainly in recent times the name has been changed so often that the basic reason for having a name, so that people can refer to it simply and unambiguously, is completely lost. The name *elata* means 'elevated', possibly referring to the height, although the trees are not extremely tall.

River peppermint is found on the eastern parts of the central tablelands and the south coast of New South Wales, and the eastern parts of Victoria. It is most common along the banks of rivers, but is also found in undulating country where the rainfall and soil type provide adequate moisture without water-logging.

This species is normally a medium-sized tree, with a stocking of rough, grey bark, often cracked into roughly rectangular scales, and smooth, white bark on the upper trunk and branches. The long, narrow leaves and open crown cast a light shade, whilst the flowers and fruits are produced in abundance. The buds are small and club-shaped, but are borne in umbels of up to thirty, so that when they flower, from winter to spring, each umbel becomes a dense ball of stamens.

E. elata has been planted as an ornamental, and grows rapidly under suitable conditions. It is frost-hardy but, in Australia, is often attacked by leaf-eating beetles. The foliage is sometimes used for oil distillation.

PLATE 173

ROBERTSON'S PEPPERMINT (*Eucalyptus robertsonii*)

This tree has a more restricted natural distribution than most of the peppermints, being mainly confined to the southern highlands of New South Wales, but occurring also to a limited extent in eastern Victoria. Its main occurrence is above 2,000 feet altitude, but in Victoria it is closer to sea level.

Although it is sometimes found on shallow soils, it thrives in cool, moist sites, and tolerates moderate frosts and occasional falls of snow. In this type of country it grows to 180 feet, and up to five feet in diameter.

E. robertsonii is closely related to the narrow-leaved peppermint (*E. radiata*), and has a similar persistent, closely fibrous, dark grey bark. The main difference between these species is that *E. robertsonii* has grey-green adult leaves which are generally shorter than those of *E. radiata*.

This species has been planted occasionally in New Zealand where it makes a very good shade tree for farmlands. The crown is rather dense and spreading

when grown under these conditions, although in natural growth it tends to be only of moderate size. It flowers in late summer.

As is typical of the peppermints, this species has copious oil glands in the leaves, multi-flowered umbels of small, club-shaped buds, and rather small, pear-shaped or ovoid fruits with a flat top.

This species was named by W. F. Blakely in honour of C. C. Robertson of the Forest Department, Pretoria, the author of a book on the forest trees of Australia.

PLATE 174

BLACK PEPPERMINT (*Eucalyptus amygdalina*)

In 1792 Labillardière collected specimens of a peppermint which he later named *E. amygdalina*. Since he touched only Tasmania, in south-eastern Australia, this specimen must have been collected there. Seeds of this species were distributed and planted in various parts of Europe, and other names were applied to it, but further confusion arose because several other species, from the mainland of Australia, were also identified with this name, or regarded as varieties. At present, *E. amygdalina* is usually applied only to the common, rough-barked peppermint of Tasmania.

The name *amygdalina* refers to a fancied resemblance to the almond tree. It is usually only a small tree, sometimes with the branches smooth but otherwise covered by dark grey, closely fibrous bark. The leaves vary from narrowly lanceolate to linear, and green to slightly greyish. Supposed hybrids between this and several related trees have been recorded.

Black peppermint is widespread and abundant throughout the eastern half of Tasmania, growing on shallow acid soils, and flowering in summer.

PLATE 175

NARROW-LEAVED PEPPERMINT (*Eucalyptus radiata*)

Closely related to black peppermint (*E. amygdalina*) and Robertson's peppermint (*E. robertsonii*), this species is widespread in central and eastern Victoria and in New South Wales south coastal areas and the adjacent lower mountains, extending inland as far as Oberon in the central highlands. Its best development is in the moist forests, on moderately deep soils, preferring those with a sandy topsoil but clay subsoil. It is often seen as a woodland tree, on soils derived from basalt in the cool, moist region. Here it has a short bole and wide-spreading crown of narrow, dark green leaves. Because of its dense shade and its ability to stand lopping, it is a valuable farmland shelter tree. It flowers from spring to summer.

Narrow-leaved peppermint is one of the species which have been used for commercial distillation of oil. There are large variations in the type of oil which different trees yield, however, and one variety, var. *australiana*, has been distinguished on the presence of large quantities of cineol, which is used in the pharmaceutical industry.

E. radiata also has a persistent, finely fibrous bark, multi-flowered umbels of small, club-shaped buds and small, ovoid fruits with narrow, flat rims and small valves. The name *radiata* means 'rayed', referring to the ray-like appearance of the plentiful buds. The long, narrow leaves have a conspicuous intramarginal vein, and often a second such vein runs the length of the leaf.

PLATE 176

BROAD-LEAVED PEPPERMINT (*Eucalyptus dives*)

Distinctive amongst the peppermints in having large, ovate, stem-clasping juvenile leaves which are blue-grey and conspicuous in the undergrowth, broad-leaved peppermint is very easy to identify in areas where eucalyptus oil distillation operations have been carried out, for this is one of the species used, and it coppices vigorously from the waist-high stumps. The name *dives* means 'rich' or 'plentiful', referring to the quantities of oil in the plant. However, it is not used as extensively as narrow-leaved peppermint (*E. radiata*) for this purpose.

E. dives is widespread in eastern and southern Victoria, especially on the foothills of the Dividing Range. In New South Wales it is common on the south-western slopes and on the southern and central tablelands, extending in altitude from 500 to 4,000 feet. It is commonly found on poor, shallow soils and infertile, stony slopes, in regions of mild climate, but will withstand moderate frosts. It flowers in spring.

The bark of this species is typical of the peppermints, being persistent on the trunk and large branches, but smooth on the upper part of the tree. This is generally a small tree, seldom reaching eighty feet in height and usually has a large crown of glossy, dark green, elliptical or lanceolate leaves.

These are rather thick, with copious oil dots, and have conspicuous venation at an acute angle to the midrib.

PLATE 177

TASMANIAN SNOW GUM (*Eucalyptus coccifera*)

On the highest and bleakest sites, Tasmanian snow gum, like its relative, snow gum (*E. pauciflora*), on the mainland, is reduced to a shrub or stunted tree, with a short, twisted stem and wind-swept branches. At lower altitudes and more favourable sites, however, it becomes a larger tree of better form, reaching eighty feet in height.

The bark of this tree is shed in long strips leaving a smooth, white or irregularly blotched, grey and white surface. The rather open crown is made up of short, thick leaves, usually lanceolate with a fine, hooked point. The smaller branches are covered with a waxy surface, especially at higher altitudes.

Usually in groups of three but occasionally up to five, the buds are wrinkled, with a low operculum and tapering calyx tube, and the flowers occur in summer. The fruits are very similar to those of snow gum, being rather large and woody, short-stalked and conic or hemispheric with a wide, flat disc.

E. coccifera is one of the most cold-hardy of the eucalypts and will stand temperatures close to 0°F. Its botanical name was intended to refer to the presence of coccids or scale insects on the twigs, but, unhappily, this is a common feature of many of the eucalypts, so the name is not especially appropriate.

PLATE 178

SILVER PEPPERMINT (*Eucalyptus tenuiramis*)

This tree is widespread and abundant in the south and south-east of Tasmania, from sea level to 1,500 feet, often forming pure stands on dry, mudstone hills. *E. tenuiramis* is a tree of up to eighty feet, sometimes with pendulous branches, and usually glaucous, but there is some variation in this feature. This species was originally described as *E. tenuiramis* by Miquel from fragmentary material which is now held at the herbarium of the State University of Utrecht, in Holland, and there was some confusion as to the application of the name, whilst Blakely renamed the silver peppermint as *E. tasmanica*, a name which should now be regarded as synonymous with *E. tenuiramis*.

The bark of this tree is deciduous, smooth and

light grey. It has brown timber which is moderately durable in the ground.

Silver peppermint has been grown successfully in New Zealand, where it is able to withstand considerable exposure and is a useful species for windbreaks on cold sites. It flowers profusely from spring to early summer.

The word *tenuiramis* means 'slender branches'.

PLATE 179

NEW ENGLAND BLACKBUTT (*Eucalyptus campanulata*)

This is a medium-sized tree of the cool, moist region which runs in a narrow belt between the coastal lowlands and the tablelands of northern New South Wales. This country was, until relatively recently, difficult to exploit because of its rather rugged topography, and New England blackbutt was not well known.

It is a tree of good form, with persistent, finely fibrous bark on the trunk and lower branches but with smooth, white branches and a well-developed crown of curved, bright green leaves. The juvenile leaves are rather broad, oblique and ash-grey.

E. campanulata was named by Baker and Smith, the name referring to the bell-shaped fruit, although, as in many other eucalypts, there is considerable variation in fruit shape and often it would be better described as pear-shaped.

This species occurs principally in good quality forest, on rather steep country and usually on fertile, loamy soils, although it is often found on coarse, sandy loams derived from granite. The area has warm summers and cool to cold winters, with a reliable, fairly uniformly distributed rainfall, or with slightly more in summer, and up to sixty inches annually. Snow falls each winter on the highest localities.

New England blackbutt is a useful tree for timber production and should prove valuable for planting in cool, moist climates, but has not been tried extensively. It flowers during summer.

PLATE 180

SCRIBBLY GUM (*Eucalyptus haemastoma*)

On the sterile, shallow, sandy soils which have developed on the Hawkesbury sandstone near Sydney, scribbly gum grows as a small tree with a light, irregular crown and a smooth, white or pale grey bark which is marked by irregular scribbles. These scribbles are made by insect larvae burrowing beneath the bark, and on close examination can be seen to be a double track.

Scribbly gum may be reduced to a mere shrub on especially poor sites, and sometimes forms dense thickets. The thick, leathery leaves are usually curved, with rather acute lateral veins.

The botanical name, meaning 'red opening', refers to the reddish-coloured, flat or slightly convex disc on the top of the fruit. Although not restricted to this species, the red disc is fairly conspicuous and is a good indicator.

Apart from the fact that it will grow on extremely poor sites in a mild climate, scribbly gum has little to recommend it. The timber is of no commercial value. Flowering can be in spring to summer or sometimes in autumn.

PLATE 181

NARROW-LEAVED RED MALLEE (*Eucalyptus foecunda*)

A common mallee with a climatic range from eight to thirty inches annual rainfall, this species occurs from southern Western Australia, through South Australia to western Victoria and New South Wales. It is almost invariably a compact, many-stemmed mallee from six to fifteen feet; occasionally an individual in a favoured position will attain twenty or thirty feet. The slender stems are rough, dark grey, with bark shedding in strips for a few feet at the base, and smooth, red-brown or grey-brown bark higher up.

The conical buds are often bright red or yellow, and are prolifically produced. The abundance of flowers and fruits is remarked by the name *foecunda* which means 'fruitful'.

The narrow-leaved red mallee grows in sandy soil in flat areas of low scrub. It flowers from January to March, and would be an extremely attractive garden shrub in most gardens. It would also be an ideal windbreak species. It is drought-resistant and moderately frost-resistant.

PLATE 182

WHITE-LEAVED MALLEE (*Eucalyptus albida*)

Juvenile leaves of most species of *Eucalyptus* are very distinctive, but none more so than those of *E. albida*. It is called the white-leaved mallee, and the name *albida* refers to whiteness, all alluding to the creamy white, opposite leaves of juvenile shoots on the plants. Mostly these white leaves are low on the mallee, but sometimes an upper branch has reversionary, white, oval leaves. The ordinary, or adult leaves are narrowly lanceolate, alternate, and light green.

The white-leaved mallee grows to about ten feet high, with smooth, grey or brown bark. It occurs in sandy or lateritic soil in the low, open, heath-like scrub in the area including Newdegate, Kondinin, Harrismith and Hyden, in Western Australia.

Flowering in winter, *E. albida* is drought- and frost-resistant, admirably suitable for planting in shrubberies or for windbreaks, and the white leaves are useful in floral arrangements.

PLATE 183

HOOK-LEAVED MALLEE (*Eucalyptus uncinata*)

The name *uncinata* means 'barbed', a reference to the tip of the leaf which is mostly turned like a hook, and thus the common name is a translation of the botanical name. The hooked leaf is not unique to this species, however, but it is a help in identification. Also useful is the feature of the filaments which are bent sharply inwards from near the middle. The buds are attractive, being abundant and often orange or reddish, with very short or no individual stalks. The flowers occur from February to April.

Hook-leaved mallee is always a mallee, mostly about six feet high, but occasionally taller, with thin, smooth, grey or brown stems. It grows naturally in gravelly sand or sandy loam mainly in the extreme southern area of Western Australia, and extending through the drier country to the Eyre Peninsula of South Australia, although it is not common in the latter State.

E. uncinata is drought-resistant and moderately frost-resistant, being particularly useful as an attractive windbreak or hedge in sandy soils in rainfalls of from ten to twenty inches annually.

PLATE 184

CRIMSON MALLEE BOX (*Eucalyptus lansdowneana* var. *lansdowneana*)

Native to Kangaroo Island and from Port Lincoln to Gawler in South Australia, this is also known as crimson mallee, red-flowered mallee, red mallee and Port Lincoln mallee. Flowers in December to

February can be creamy, pink, red, mauve or almost purple. The species can be a mallee or small tree up to twelve or fifteen feet high, with drooping branches; the bark is rough and flaky at the base of the trunk and smooth grey above.

E. lansdowneana is named after Thomas Lansdowne Brown, one of the first collectors of the species, and it has been in cultivation as an ornamental for many years. It is drought- and frost-resistant, able to grow adequately in areas of ten inch annual rainfall, and can make a useful windbreak. In California it grew twelve feet in three years. In cultivation it is usually compact and is suitable for hedges.

Some distinctive features are the flowers virtually without individual stalks, and the barrel-shaped fruits with two or four faint, longitudinal ridges.

PLATE 185

WHITE-FLOWERED MALLEE (*Eucalyptus lansdowneana* var. *leucantha*)

The varietal name *leucantha* refers to white filaments. This is a naturally-occurring white or creamy-flowered form of the crimson mallee box (*E. lansdowneana* var. *lansdowneana*), found in South Australia at Port Lincoln and Encounter Bay, and probably elsewhere.

As there is much variation in the colour of flowers of some species of *Eucalyptus*, such varieties as this one are usually not recognised in botanical classification, but there is some convenience in using the name for the white-flowering form.

In habit it is identical to the crimson mallee box, forming a shrubby plant to about fifteen feet high, and flowering from December until about May. It is resistant to frost and drought, and is suitable for windbreaks.

PLATE 186

QUORN MALLEE (*Eucalyptus porosa*)

This mallee, mainly from South Australia, is part of a complex group which has not been separated satisfactorily. It intergrades with the peppermint box (*E. odorata* var. *odorata*) and small-fruited forms of yellow gum (*E. leucoxylon* var. *leucoxylon*). It has been regarded by various botanists as a form of the black mallee-box (*E. calcicultrix*), as a variety worthy of a name, and as a separate species.

The Quorn mallee usually grows as a mallee, or

sometimes as a small tree, with black, scaly bark on the trunk and smooth branches. Its main features of distinction from *E. calcicultrix* are the narrower leaves and small buds with obtuse caps.

The species occurs in southern South Australia up to the Flinders Ranges, and into New South Wales near Broken Hill. It flowers mainly in winter.

PLATE 187

PEPPERMINT BOX (*Eucalyptus odorata* var. *odorata*)

Both the common name and the botanical name of this species refer to the scent of the leaves when they are crushed. The scent is due to the large quantities of oils, mostly cineol, which they contain.

E. odorata was once the principal eucalypt on the plains where Adelaide now stands. It is distributed over a wide area of South Australia from the Bight and Eyre Peninsula eastwards to the Flinders Ranges and south-east to Kangaroo Island with a small occurrence in south-eastern South Australia and western Victoria. Over this range it varies considerably in form, from a tree up to fifty feet in height with rough, dark brown bark, to a slender mallee or a shrub. It is frequently a mallee of moderate size with a large lignotuber, or a much-branched, irregular tree.

The region of its occurrence has a Mediterranean type of climate, with cool, wet winters and hot, dry summers. The annual rainfall is usually between fifteen and thirty inches.

The leaves of peppermint box are normally dark green on both surfaces and have rather prominent venation; light green and greyish forms are also seen.

Peppermint box flowers during summer.

PLATE 188

SEASIDE MALLEE (*Eucalyptus odorata* var. *angustifolia*)

The leaves of this variety are generally narrower than those of the typical variety (*E. odorata* var. *odorata*), as implied by the name *angustifolia*, meaning 'narrow-leaved'.

This is generally a mallee, with a few feet of rough bark at the base of the stems, occurring in the Eyre Peninsula and the Flinders Ranges, in South Australia.

Flowers are reported in spring and in autumn.

PLATE 189

BLUE MALLEE (*Eucalyptus fruticetorum*)

This species occurs on the western slopes of the Dividing Range in New South Wales, being common near Wyalong. It also occurs in Victoria from near Bendigo to Mildura.

Blue mallee is one of the most important of the mallees for oil production, particularly in the Bendigo district.

It occurs on both sandy and clay soils, growing to twenty feet, with smooth, light-coloured stems and blue-grey, narrow leaves.

Blue mallee flowers irregularly, from March to June and in spring, and serves as a useful source of both honey and pollen.

This species is regarded by some authors as the same as *E. odorata* var. *angustifolia*.

PLATE 190

GREEN MALLEE (*Eucalyptus viridis*)

Green mallee is found in the northern part of Victoria, and in New South Wales, particularly on the western slopes, with a small occurrence near Inglewood in Queensland.

It has very narrow, green leaves, a feature which distinguishes it from blue mallee (*E. fruticetorum*): the name *viridis* means 'green', emphasising this feature.

E. viridis forms small trees, up to thirty feet tall, but is typically a whipstick mallee, growing in dense thickets on loamy soils or stony ridges. Usually less than fifteen feet tall, with stems two to three inches in diameter, green mallee has dark brown, scaly, bark at the base of the stems but smooth white bark on the upper part. It coppices freely when cut.

Green mallee is one of the species which have been used for oil distillation, the leaves yielding about one per cent of oil with a high percentage of cineol. It flowers profusely at irregular intervals.

PLATE 191

THOZET'S BOX (*Eucalyptus thozetiana*)

Thozet's box occurs in Queensland, from near the Tropic of Capricorn, 100 to 250 miles west of Rockhampton, southwards through central Queensland to the New South Wales border. It is also found in central Australia, about fifty miles east of Alice Springs, the two areas being separated by hundreds of miles of *Acacia* woodland, grasslands and desert.

In central Australia it is only a small tree, below forty feet tall, with a short trunk and an open crown of long, ascending branches. On more favourable sites it grows to eighty feet in height, and up to three feet in diameter. It has a smooth, light-coloured bark, which is shed in small flakes except for a few feet at the base of the trunk.

E. thozetiana commonly occurs on quartzite or sandstone hills and undulating country. The area of its distribution has a ten to twenty-five inch rainfall, with a summer maximum in the moister, eastern areas, but very irregular in the inland locality. Temperatures often exceed one hundred degrees in summer, but there are occasional frosts in winter.

Thozet's box is an attractive tree which may be useful for windbreak or shade-tree planting in dry regions. It flowers in winter or early spring.

This species is named after M. Thozet who collected the species in Queensland. It is sometimes known by the aboriginal name 'yapunyah'.

PLATE 192

NARROW-LEAVED BOX (*Eucalyptus pilligaensis*)

This species was named by J. H. Maiden in reference to the Pilliga Scrub area of rather dry forest, in the north-central part of New South Wales, where it is a common tree. It extends north-east from this area to the Inglewood district of southern Queensland.

E. pilligaensis is a medium-sized tree, up to eighty feet tall, with a finely fibrous, light or medium grey bark over the trunk and large branches, the small branches being smooth. The very fine foliage is distinctive amongst the boxes although some other species have fairly narrow leaves. Flowers are seen in winter or spring. It grows on low-lying land, on both sandy and loamy soils, in a region where the rainfall of fifteen to twenty-five inches tends to have maxima in winter and summer, with dry spring and autumn. Temperatures commonly exceed one hundred degrees in summer, whilst there are occasional frosts in winter.

PLATE 193

BLACK BOX (*Eucalyptus largiflorens*)

Black box is a small tree, usually less than sixty feet tall, with an open, irregular crown of dull green, and a hard, rugged, dark grey bark on the trunk and large branches. It is widely distributed along the watercourses of western New South Wales, extending into southern Queensland, northern Victoria, and near the Murray River in South Australia. In this area it is usually found on slightly higher ground than the river red gum (*E. camaldulensis*), or forming a rather open woodland formation without any other species of eucalypt occurring there.

On the heavy, grey clays which are periodically flooded, black box relies partly on moisture stored in the soil to enable it to survive the dry summers, for these regions usually have less than fifteen inches of rain annually, and droughts are common.

This tree was known by the botanical name of *E. bicolor*, a name used by Alan Cunningham for a tree with both pink and white flowers, which he found in the Lachlan region of New South Wales. His description was published by Hooker in 1848 but was not considered specific enough to enable later botanists to be certain that he was referring to the black box, however, and von Mueller's name *E. largiflorens* is now generally accepted. This botanical name means 'large and glittering', which, von Mueller says, is 'expressive of the exuberance of its flowers'; the flowers occur from spring to summer.

Black box is frost- and drought-resistant, but grows slowly and does not seem to be a very vigorous tree. It does not withstand fires or grazing.

PLATE 194

COAST GREY BOX (*Eucalyptus bosistoana*)

Occurring in Victoria from near Bairnsdale to east Gippsland, and along the south coast of New South Wales to just north of Penrith, the coast grey box is found on a range of soils from heavy, periodically waterlogged clays to better quality clay loams on higher ground. On the wetter sites it may be only a small, shrubby tree, but in other places trees of 160 feet have been recorded.

Coast grey box sometimes occurs with the closely similar grey box (*E. moluccana*), one difference being that the wood of the latter turns grey when cut, whilst that of *E. bosistoana* stays yellow for a long time. The juvenile leaves of the latter are also thinner in texture, while the adult leaves are usually narrower. Buds and fruits also differ from grey box, the fruits of *E. bosistoana* being distinctive in usually having six valves.

The bark of the coast grey box is persistent at the base of the trunk, dark grey and softly fibrous, whilst the upper part and the branches are smooth and white, or light grey.

Coast grey box is typically a forest tree, with a tall, straight trunk and rather erect, open crown. It has hard, very strong and durable timber and is used for heavy construction work. Flowering in summer, it produces good quality honey.

This species was named by Ferdinand von Mueller in honour of Joseph Bosisto, an industrial chemist who investigated many of the products of the eucalypts during the nineteenth century.

PLATE 195

BROAD-LEAVED MALLEE BOX (*Eucalyptus behriana*)

This species has a wide distribution, from Kangaroo Island and Eyre Peninsula in South Australia, through western Victoria and as far south as Bacchus Marsh, west of Melbourne, and in the Wyalong district of New South Wales.

Usually a mallee, *E. behriana* sometimes grows as a small tree, up to thirty-five feet tall, with a smooth, cream, light grey or oily green bark surface. The large, thick, shiny leaves, with conspicuous venation, are distinctive. The inflorescence, with flowers in summer, is usually a panicle at the end of the branch-let, and in this and the general appearance of the buds and fruits, this species resembles the grey box (*E. moluccana*).

Dr Hermann Behr was a botanical collector in South Australia about the middle of the nineteenth century.

PLATE 196

NARROW-LEAVED GREY BOX (*Eucalyptus woollsiana*)

With its close resemblance to the inland grey box (*E. microcarpa*), especially to some of the narrow-leaved forms of the latter, *E. woollsiana* forms one end of a chain of related species, which are very valuable trees for shade, shelter, firewood and fencing materials. They all have hard, heavy, tough and durable timbers, and, growing mostly in the wood-lands on the inland slopes of the Dividing Range, are very useful for the grazing industry.

Narrow-leaved grey box is regarded by some authorities as a form of *E. microcarpa*. Both have closely fibrous, dark grey bark on the trunk and larger branches but smooth bark on the smaller bran-ches. *E. woollsiana* usually has narrower leaves and extends further inland and slightly further into Queensland than does *E. microcarpa*.

This species was named by R. T. Baker to honour the Rev. W. Woolls, an enthusiastic amateur botanist who was responsible for the recognition of a number of new species of *Eucalyptus* in New South Wales.

The species may flower from late summer until spring.

PLATE 197

INLAND GREY BOX (*Eucalyptus microcarpa*)

This species forms one part of a closely related group, the grey boxes, which intergrade and are very diffi-cult to separate in some localities, although over much of the range of each they are distinct. *E. microcarpa* is sometimes regarded as a small-fruited variety of the common grey box (*E. moluccana*) of coastal New South Wales and Queensland. It occupies a different area, however, being common over an extensive region on the inland side of the Dividing Range from southern Queensland through New South Wales to Victoria and with a limited occurrence in the Flinders Ranges of South Australia.

E. microcarpa, as the name implies, has smaller fruits than *E. moluccana*, but is similar in appearance. It has a dark grey, finely fibrous bark on the trunk and larger branches, but smooth, light grey or cream bark on the branches. The crown is rather upright and the leaves vary from narrowly lanceolate to elliptical. In this feature it forms a link between *E. moluccana* which has broad, thick leaves and *E. woollsiana* which has uniformly narrow leaves.

This is a woodland species, growing up to eighty feet tall, usually on heavy soils in a warm to hot, rather dry, climate, and flowering from late summer through winter until early spring.

PLATE 198

GREY BOX (*Eucalyptus moluccana*)

This is another species which has suffered a change in its botanical name in recent years, to conform with the International Code for Botanical Nomenclature. For many years it was known as *E. hemiphloia*, a name which means 'half-barked', and which seemed appro-priate. This name was published in 1867 by Bentham, however, and must give way to the earlier name *E. moluccana*, published originally by Roxburgh in Hortus Bengalensis, in 1814, without a description, and giving 'Moluccas' as the place of origin. How-ever, a type specimen is held in the British Museum of Natural History, and there is no doubt that this name applies to the grey box.

This tree is common on clay soils on the eastern coast of Australia between Sydney and Rockhampton in Queensland. It is a distinctive tree, flowering in summer and autumn, and growing mainly in open forests or tall woodlands, where it has a trunk of about half the total height, and an upright, branching habit, with a moderately dense crown. The bark on the trunk is rough, grey, and adheres closely to the stem. It is shed from the branches in long strips which often hang from the upper branches, leaving a smooth, light grey surface.

The large, ovate, leathery juvenile leaves are medium to dark green, with a conspicuous intramarginal vein. The adult leaves are thick, green and glossy on both surfaces.

Grey box is highly regarded as a timber tree, producing strong, durable timber which is also very good firewood.

PLATE 199

WHITE BOX (*Eucalyptus albens*)

E. albens has an appropriate name, for it gives the impression of being a white tree, although when examined more closely, few of its features are really white. Perhaps the closest is the inflorescence, for the long buds with sharply conic opercula, and the stalks, are covered with a white, powdery wax. The twigs and leaves are also white to grey-green, and the closely adherent, finely fibrous bark is light grey-brown or very pale grey. Seen from a distance, the pale trunk and silver crown are very distinctive.

The rounded crown and large, rather broadly lanceolate leaves give an appearance of solidity to the tree, and the shade it casts is quite dense. This is a good shade and shelter tree in its native environment, which includes much of the wheatlands of New South Wales, along the western side of the Dividing Range, and in the upper Hunter River valley; to the south it extends into the northern part of Victoria and has a limited occurrence in South Australia.

White box occurs on fairly rich, well-drained soils of both igneous and sedimentary origin. It grows to over eighty feet in height, often with a bole about half the height of the tree. It is moderately resistant to frost and drought, and flowers from late summer sometimes into winter.

PLATE 200

BIMBLE BOX (*Eucalyptus populnea*)

A fairly common tree in inland parts of south-eastern Queensland and north-eastern New South Wales, bimble box is found mainly on heavy clay soils which tend to be waterlogged in the wet season, but occurs on a variety of other sites. It grows to about eighty feet in height, with a relatively short bole and a compact crown made up of circular or broadly elliptical leaves which are shining green and carried on rather long, slender petioles. These leaves are referred to by the name *populnea*, meaning 'like a poplar'.

The bark is persistent to the small branches, finely interwoven and short-fibred. It is light grey-brown, or often has patches of slightly darker brown and light grey. The timber of this species is heavy and durable, makes good firewood but is difficult to split.

Bimble box suckers freely when felled, and is rather difficult to eradicate from farm land. It provides good shade and shelter, however, and is an attractive tree for heavy soils, flowering in late summer.

PLATE 201

COOLIBAH (*Eucalyptus microtheca*)

This is the species mentioned by A. B. 'Banjo' Paterson in the famous poem 'Waltzing Matilda':

'Once a jolly swagman camped by a billabong
    Under the shade of a coolibah tree'

This sums up some of the tree's characteristics, for it is a shady tree if growing near a billabong, or seasonal water. For much of the year, however, coolibah has dry conditions. It occurs in the arid parts of mainland Australia near watercourses or on flats where there is periodic inundation.

Old coolibah trees can be quite gnarled and spreading, but on clayey flats the trees are thinner and more erect. The bark can be smooth grey or white, or it may be rough, fibrous grey on the trunk and smooth grey above. The small fruits and pendulous leaves are typical of the coolibah, which flowers in winter or spring.

The word 'coolibah', an aboriginal name, is sometimes spelt 'coolabah', and the species has also been known as flooded box. The timber, though only small in length, is hard and durable, and has been used for shafts, wheels, fencing and fuel.

Coolibah eventually makes a tree full of character with irregular shape. It is extremely drought- and frost-resistant and can withstand inundation. It has been planted in Arizona, United States of America.

The name *microtheca* means 'a small case or container', and therefore this is a reference to the small fruiting capsules which contain the seeds.

PLATE 202

NARROW-LEAVED RED IRONBARK
(*Eucalyptus crebra*)

This species has the widest distribution of any ironbark and extends over twenty degrees of latitude, from near Cairns in tropical Queensland to a little south of Sydney. In Queensland it is common in a belt from 200 to nearly 300 miles wide, from the coast to just over the Great Dividing Range. In New South Wales the main occurrence is inland, near Baradine, but it also occurs near the coast in the Sydney area. With such a wide geographic distribution it can be expected to be tolerant to a wide range of climate and soils; the soils vary from clays to acid, sandy surface soils over clay subsoil. The botanical name means 'crowded', referring to the abundant occurrence of the species.

Narrow-leaved red ironbark is usually only a medium-sized tree, rarely reaching one hundred feet, and has hard, furrowed bark to the small branches. The bark is usually dark grey and densely impregnated with reddish-brown gum.

This species has both narrow juvenile leaves and narrow adult leaves, which are dull green or grey-green on both surfaces. The small, cream flowers are produced from winter to summer in panicles at the ends of the branchlets and the small, ovoid fruits have enclosed valves.

PLATE 203

LEMON-SCENTED IRONBARK (*Eucalyptus staigerana*)

Named in honour of Karl Staiger, Government analytical chemist of Queensland during part of the nineteenth century, lemon-scented ironbark is interesting mainly because the leaves contain oils which Staiger considered to resemble verbena oil. The major constituent is limonene, but the lemon scent is due to citral. The tree was discovered by P. F. Sellheim, named by Ferdinand von Mueller, and the description published by F. Manson Bailey in his *Synopsis of the Queensland Flora*, in 1883.

This is a medium-sized tree, similar to the narrow-leaved red ironbark (*E. crebra*), but with broader juvenile leaves and mostly broader adult leaves which

are lemon-scented. The hard, dark grey bark is persistent to the smaller branches and the small, cream flowers are borne in axillary umbels or terminal panicles, mainly in summer.

E. staigerana occurs naturally in a relatively restricted area in northern Queensland, in the vicinity of the Palmer River.

PLATE 204

BLUE-LEAVED IRONBARK (*Eucalyptus fibrosa* ssp. *nubila*)

This tree is closely related to the broad-leaved red ironbark (*E. fibrosa* ssp. *fibrosa*) and intergrades with it in a few localities. It is distinguished by the waxy, blue-grey bloom on the branchlets, leaves, buds and fruits, and by the smaller leaves and fruits and shorter operculum.

Blue-leaved ironbark occurs in the inland parts of south-eastern Queensland, near Dubbo and Dunedoo in the central western slopes region of New South Wales, and farther east in the Goulburn valley to near Merriwa. It occurs on sandy soils, stony ridges or on areas subject to waterlogging. The tree is moderately ornamental, although it rarely grows to a large size. Flowering is in summer.

This species was originally called *E. siderophloia* var. *glauca*, when it was described by Deane and Maiden, in 1899. By 1933, however, Maiden regarded it as a separate species and called it *E. nubilis*. L. Johnson considered this to be a misspelling for *nubila* (*nubilis* means 'marriageable'; *nubila* means 'dusky'), and at the same time reunited it with the broad-leaved red ironbark which he considers should be called *E. fibrosa*.

PLATE 205

BROAD-LEAVED RED IRONBARK
(*Eucalyptus fibrosa* ssp. *fibrosa*)

The broad-leaved red ironbark is found mainly along the coast of New South Wales and south-eastern Queensland, from south of Bateman's Bay to near Rockhampton, with the major occurrence between Brisbane and Maryborough. There are also small areas where it occurs on the western slopes of New South Wales and adjacent areas in Queensland.

This is typically a species of heavy soils in areas of moderate rainfall and mild to hot climates. Most of the area is almost frost-free, and in the inland parts maximum temperatures in summer commonly exceed one hundred degrees F. Growing on relatively flat or undulating country, *E. fibrosa* may reach one hundred feet in height, with a bole of about half the total height, and moderate to poor form. It frequently has a large, open crown.

The bark of this species is rather softer and more flaky than the typical ironbark. It is dark brown to almost black and usually impregnated with reddish-brown gum. The name *E. fibrosa* is based on specimens collected by Ferdinand von Mueller in Queensland, but there is some doubt that this name should be applied to the broad-leaved red ironbark. The name *E. siderophloia* which was previously used for this species, means 'ironbark', but this name was based on mixed material, and is now considered to apply to a different species.

One of the distinctive features is the large, leathery, juvenile leaves. These are dull green. The adult leaves are much narrower, dark green on both surfaces and with a distinct intramarginal vein. Flowers occur in summer.

PLATE 206

SILVER BOX (*Eucalyptus pruinosa*)

Distinctive because of its silvery-grey, oval, stalkless leaves and rough, fibrous bark, the silver box grows in the fifteen to thirty-five inch rainfall zone of the Northern Territory, extending into northern Western Australia and north-western Queensland, and on to islands in the Gulf of Carpentaria. It is also known as the silver-leaved box, aptly describing the species, for the finely fibrous bark is of the type which is known as box bark. The name *pruinosa* means 'frosted', a reference to the frosty appearance of the leaves, as shown in the painting.

Silver box is a small tree usually up to twenty feet, but sometimes as high as thirty feet. It grows on flat areas of shallow, red, sandy soil, sometimes calcareous, and also on some rocky limestone areas. It flowers in winter.

Drought-resistant, but probably frost-tender at least when young, the silver box could be an attractive small tree in tropical areas, and it is a useful firewood species.

PLATE 207

SILVER-LEAVED IRONBARK (*Eucalyptus melanophloia*)

The name *melanophloia* means 'black bark', which refers to the hard, black, furrowed ironbark of this species.

Silver-leaved ironbark is a small to medium-sized tree which is found over a wide area in northern New South Wales and eastern Queensland. In inland sites it is most common on deep, loamy soils, but in the regions of higher rainfall it is frequently the only tree on poor, stony hillsides, where its irregular trunk and twisted branches make it seem to be struggling for life.

This is one of the eucalypts which retains its intermediate, opposite-leaved foliage throughout its life, the adult leaves being rarely seen. The leaves are opposite and sessile, broadly ovate and grey-green to silvery blue. The buds are borne in umbels of seven in the axils of the upper leaves. They are also silver, whilst the stamens, when the flowers appear in summer, are cream.

Silver-leaved ironbark is a relatively slow-growing tree in its native habitat. It is drought-resistant and provides good shade and shelter.

PLATE 208

GUM-TOPPED BOX (*Eucalyptus orgadophila*)

This is not a well-known species, as it occurs in a few localities on the inland side of the Dividing Range, in south-eastern Queensland, in areas which are rather sparsely populated. The main occurrence is to the north and north-west of Dalby, but specimens have also been collected from near Warwick. The name *orgadophila* means 'meadow-loving', probably a reference to the habitat where the species was first collected. A small tree, growing to about forty feet in height, *E. orgadophila* is similar to yellow box (*E. melliodora*) in general appearance. It has closely fibrous bark on the trunk, but smooth branches. The juvenile leaves are ovate or broadly elliptical, often notched at the apex, and with a prominent intramarginal vein, whilst the adult leaves are narrow, tapering into the long petiole, and dull green with faint venation.

As in yellow box, the inflorescences of gum-topped box may be either in the axils of the leaves or at the ends of the branchlets, the white flowers, in umbels of up to seven, usually appearing in August or September. The fruits are pear-shaped, with faint ribs, and usually topped by the enlarged staminal ring. This is a feature which is also common in yellow box and in mugga (*E. sideroxylon*).

Further work is needed to show the relationship of this species to yellow box, but it appears to be potentially useful for similar purposes to that species.

PLATE 209

GREY IRONBARK (*Eucalyptus paniculata*)

A common tree in coastal New South Wales, grey ironbark has one of the hardest, heaviest, toughest, strongest, and most durable timbers in a genus renowned for timbers with these qualities. It grows to over one hundred feet, often with a trunk over sixty feet in height and up to four feet in diameter.

The name *paniculata* refers to the compound, paniculate inflorescence, which is borne at the ends of the twigs or in the axils of the upper leaves. The double-conic buds give way to pear-shaped or ovoid fruits with a narrow disc and short valves, and the tree flowers mainly in summer.

Grey ironbark occurs on a wide range of topography from valley floors, where it makes its best growth, to the slopes and tops of ridges and hills. It will grow on poor, stony soils, but is commonly found on clay loams or sandy loams with a clay subsoil.

The adult leaves are oblong to lanceolate, and dark green on the upper surface but paler on the under side. The bark is persistent to the small branches, hard, deeply furrowed and ridged, dark grey and impregnated with reddish-brown gum.

PLATE 210

CALEY'S IRONBARK (*Eucalyptus caleyi*)

Caley's ironbark is a medium-sized tree found on the north-western slopes of the Dividing Range in New South Wales, and on the lower parts of the adjacent tablelands and the upper parts of the Hunter valley.

Its black, deeply furrowed, hard bark and its silver-grey leaves make this a conspicuous tree in the forest. It is similar in appearance to the blue-leaved ironbark (*E. fibrosa* ssp. *nubila*), but the bark is harder and the buds and fruits are a different shape.

The buds are perhaps the most distinctive feature for separating this species from the other ironbarks. The operculum is conic and narrower than the calyx tube, which often appears widest below the junction with the operculum. The fruits are pear-shaped, tapering into the slender pedicels. Although the buds are often glaucous, the fruits are usually glossy brown when ripe. The tree flowers in late winter.

Caley's ironbark is named in honour of George Caley who was botanical collector for Sir Joseph Banks from 1800 to 1810.

PLATE 211

MUGGA (*Eucalyptus sideroxylon* ssp. *sideroxylon*)

Occurring over a wide area of the inland of New South Wales and adjacent parts of Victoria, with smaller occurrences in Queensland, coastal New South Wales and eastern Victoria, mugga, or red ironbark as it is often called, is a typical ironbark, with perhaps the hardest, most deeply furrowed and blackest bark of the group. The inland area of occurrence is in a rainfall region of fifteen to twenty-five inches a year, characterised by high summer temperatures, with maxima often over one hundred degrees F, and up to twenty frosts each winter. Growing in such a climate, on poor, shallow soils, *E. sideroxylon* is obviously a tough tree. It is also quite an attractive tree in cultivation, with its hard, black bark and soft, grey-green foliage. Some forms also produce bright red flowers but the colour varies through pink to cream in different trees. The glaucousness of the leaves also varies considerably.

The inland form is seven-flowered, whilst the coastal form is three-flowered, with larger flowers and fruits and glossy, green leaves. This has been recognised by L. Johnson as subspecies *tricarpa*.

The name *sideroxylon* means 'iron wood'.

Flowering time may vary according to the seed source, but can be over much of the year from winter into summer.

PLATE 212

YELLOW GUM (*Eucalyptus leucoxylon* var. *leucoxylon*)

The most important occurrence of this species is in the north-central region of Victoria, but it also occurs in the western parts of that State, and in South Australia as far north as Port Augusta. Yellow gum grows on land between near sea level—on Kangaroo Island—and nearly 2,000 feet, in climates which are temperate but often have very hot summers. Rainfall is from ten to thirty inches a year, mainly in winter, and up to fifteen frosts may occur each winter.

Yellow gum grows mainly on clay soils, usually on gently undulating to hilly country, but it is also found on the higher slopes of hills and on alluvial flats. It is a moderate-sized tree, usually less than one hundred feet tall, and with a trunk about half the total height. The crown tends to be open and relatively large.

This species is related to the ironbarks, and occasionally appears to hybridise with mugga (*E. sideroxylon* ssp. *sideroxylon*). It normally sheds the bark from the trunk and branches in irregular, roughly oval sheets, leaving the surface smooth, mottled yellow or white and blue-grey. The name *leucoxylon* means 'white wood'. Sometimes some bark is retained at the base; this is hard, deeply furrowed and grey. Flowering is from winter to summer.

PLATE 213

RED-FLOWERED YELLOW GUM (*Eucalyptus leucoxylon* var. *macrocarpa*)

This large-fruited variety of yellow gum (*E. leucoxylon* var. *leucoxylon*) occurs in several coastal districts of South Australia as a small tree, rarely growing to more than thirty feet in height. It has a smooth, yellowish bark which is shed in irregular flakes, and large, leathery leaves which are rather narrow and usually slightly curved, grey-green on both surfaces and hang vertically in a fairly open crown. The varietal name *macrocarpa* means 'large fruit'.

This variety has been widely planted as an ornamental, both in Australia and overseas. It is variable in growth, some forms being tall with a straight stem and large leaves, others growing to about six feet, with irregular stem and fine leaves. The size and colour of the flowers also vary, and seed from a single tree may produce plants with cream, pink or bright red flowers. There are forms which produce all the flowers near the ends of the branches, while others have delayed flowering so that the blossoms open on bare branches below the leaves.

Flowering time is varied as well. Most trees bloom in autumn, but often some buds remain on the tree until the following spring.

PLATE 214

SCRUBBY BLUE GUM (*Eucalyptus leucoxylon* var. *pauperita*)

This variety was described by J. E. Brown in his *Forest Flora of South Australia* in 1883, as a small-fruited form of *E. leucoxylon* var. *leucoxylon*, growing in a generally more arid environment.

For some time it was known as *E. jugalis*, but that name is now considered to apply to a hybrid which

was grown in France in the latter part of the nineteenth century.

E. leucoxylon var. *pauperita* sometimes grows to a large, spreading tree, but is more usually small, with rough, dark bark on the main trunk. It extends from the northern part of the Flinders Ranges to the Ninety Mile Desert of South Australia, and occurs also in western Victoria. This is a region where the annual rainfall is from ten to eighteen inches, with a hot, dry summer. Apart from the ability to survive in such conditions, *E. leucoxylon* var. *pauperita* appears to have few attributes which would recommend it to horticulturists. The varietal name, *pauperita*, is based on the Latin *pauper*, meaning 'poor'.

Scrubby blue gum flowers mainly from spring to early summer.

PLATE 215

YELLOW BOX (*Eucalyptus melliodora*)

Widely distributed in Victoria and New South Wales, especially on the inland side of the Dividing Range, yellow box is perhaps one of the best-known eucalypts and one which could be considered a very Australian tree. This is a species of the open forest and savannah woodland, where the trees grow far enough apart to develop large, spreading crowns and to cast a welcome shade in the hot, summer days.

Yellow box is a very useful tree, providing excellent firewood, hard, strong, durable timber, and honey which is renowned for its quality. It flowers profusely throughout the summer, although some years are much better than others. The botanical name means 'honey-scented' and is obviously appropriate.

The amount of bark retained on the trunk varies from tree to tree. Some trees are almost completely smooth with small, irregular streaks of dark and light grey; others have hard, black, scaly bark to the large branches. Most commonly, however, yellow box has a yellow-brown, sub-fibrous and rather friable bark on the trunk and large branches, while the small branches are smooth, white, cream or grey. The crown may be bright green, dull grey or almost blue.

PLATE 216

FUZZY BOX (*Eucalyptus conica*)

This species is common on the central western slopes of New South Wales, extending eastwards to the Dividing Range and northwards into Queensland, where it extends to the ill-defined divide north of Dalby.

Fuzzy box is a medium-sized tree, usually with a wide crown and pendulous branches. The bark is persistent over the trunk and branches, light grey to brown and rather softly fibrous, giving rise to the common name. The leaves are lanceolate or sometimes rather broad, dull green or greyish on both surfaces with the main veins at an acute angle to the midrib.

The most distinctive feature of fuzzy box is the shape of the fruits, which is referred to in the botanical name. These are conic, usually sessile or very short-stalked, with the valves rather deeply enclosed within the tube. The flowers occur mainly in summer.

E. conica is a useful tree for shade and shelter but the hard, red wood is difficult to split and does not burn as well as many of the other box trees, so this species is not used extensively.

PLATE 217

SLATY GUM (*Eucalyptus dawsonii*)

Slaty gum is a eucalypt of relatively restricted natural distribution, being found mainly in the Goulburn River valley, from near Muswellbrook, west to the Dividing Range, and then north-west to Pilliga in central New South Wales. In the drier parts of this region it occurs as a small to medium-sized tree in woodland formation, but in the higher parts nearer the range, it reaches 150 feet with diameters up to four feet, with a tall, straight bole.

The common name refers to the branchlets, leaves and buds which are covered with a waxy bloom and give a greyish appearance to the tree from a distance. The trunk is smooth, cream or pale blue in colour, and most attractive. The flowers, in late spring, and fruits are arranged in panicles at the ends of the branches as is typical of most of the boxes. This species is closely related to the red box (*E. polyanthemos*), and has been considered by some to be merely a variety of that species. Its red timber is hard, durable and fairly straight-grained, but is not much used because of the limited occurrence.

E. dawsonii was named after James Dawson who helped in gathering specimens of this tree and drew attention to the quality of the timber.

PLATE 218

RED BOX (*Eucalyptus polyanthemos*)

Red box is not usually a large tree, being generally less than eighty feet tall. It has a short bole and a round, often irregular crown of grey-green leaves.

This tree occurs throughout a large part of Victoria, from the Grampians to east Gippsland and along the inland slopes of the Dividing Range. It extends from the latter area into New South Wales, along the southern and central western slopes and the lower parts of the adjacent tablelands. Red box is essentially a woodland tree, but also occurs in dry forest country, particularly on stony slopes and on the heavier soils. It is rather variable in appearance, sometimes shedding all its bark to become a 'gum', at other times retaining a shortly fibrous, light brown bark to the small branches.

The juvenile leaves of red box are distinctive, being almost circular or wider than long and notched at the apex. As they are blue-grey or silver, they are most attractive and this species is cultivated both in the United States of America and in Europe, for the cut flower trade. Leaves are shipped from the south of France to London for this purpose.

E. polyanthemos is moderately hardy to frost and drought, and is a useful shade and shelter tree, with flowers in spring and summer.

The wood provides excellent firewood, and the copious flowers provide honey of moderate to good quality. The botanical name means 'many anthers', a reference to the plentiful flowers.

PLATE 219

BLUE BOX (*Eucalyptus bauerana*)

E. bauerana is a small or medium-sized tree which is found scattered throughout the coastal regions of eastern Victoria and southern New South Wales, with a few occurrences in northern New South Wales and south-eastern Queensland. It is generally on moderately good soils, and is usually conspicuous because of its dense, round crown of blue-grey leaves.

This species is related both to the red box (*E. polyanthemos*) and the fuzzy box (*E. conica*). It differs from red box in having conic fruits with a very short stalk, and from fuzzy box mainly in having broader, blue-grey leaves. It is also consistently rough-barked to the small branches, whereas red box is often smooth-barked.

E. bauerana was collected by Robert Brown, the botanist with the Flinders expedition. In 1843 specimens sent by Ferdinand Bauer to the Vienna Herbarium were used for the first formal description and it was named in honour of the collector.

This is an attractive tree for ornamental use, tolerant of light frosts and flowering in summer. It has pale brown timber which is strong and durable but is often difficult to split and does not burn readily.

PLATE 220

PINK GUM (Eucalyptus fasciculosa)

Usually less than fifty feet in height, with an irregular trunk and a rather open crown, pink gum occasionally grows as tall as eighty feet. It occurs mainly in South Australia, especially in the low hills southwards from Adelaide to Victor Harbour and on the western part of Kangaroo Island. It is less common on Eyre Peninsula and along the southern part of the border with Victoria. This is a region of cool, wet winters and warm to hot, dry summers, annual rainfall being between fifteen and thirty inches.

Pink gum, so named because of the colour of the smooth, deciduous bark, typically occurs on dry, rather sterile, hilly sites. It is a tree of woodlands or open forests, and is useful for shade and shelter on farmlands, but as it is also a good firewood, it has been cut extensively for this purpose. It is also a useful honey tree, flowering over a long period, from midsummer to late autumn.

PLATE 221

GOOSEBERRY MALLEE (Eucalyptus calycogona var. calycogona)

Very resistant to drought and frost, the gooseberry mallee grows from ten to twenty-five feet high, varying from a shapely mallee to a thin tree. It favours sandy or gravelly loam in most of the southern low rainfall area of Western Australia and extending into southern South Australia and the Flinders Ranges, and also into western Victoria. Its bark is mainly smooth grey, sometimes with some rough bark at the base of the trunks. Features to aid in identification are the pale green, shining leaves and the fruit which has four distinct corners. The name calycogona means 'cup corner', a reference to the four-angled fruits.

Gooseberry mallee is suitable for ornamental planting in arid inland areas, providing flowers from August to about November.

PLATE 222

YEELANNA MALLEE (Eucalyptus calycogona var. staffordii)

Larger buds and fruits and coarser leaves separate this variety from the gooseberry mallee (E. calycogona). This is another case where such differences are not wholly sufficient to maintain a natural variety. It is likely that a full range of variation may be found from the gooseberry mallee to the Yeelanna mallee, and yet, as in some other cases, there is some convenience in having a distinct name for a form which may be cultivated.

The Yeelanna mallee is mostly a small mallee up to twenty feet high, with smooth, grey bark, sometimes with a small quantity of rough bark at the base, and flowering from September to November, but sometimes in other months also. It has been recorded from Eyre Peninsula and Encounter Bay in South Australia.

The varietal name staffordii is actually named after W. J. Spafford who collected the first specimens. W. F. Blakely, who named the variety, misread the collector's name, and published the incorrect spelling of the name, but the published name must be maintained in this case.

PLATE 223

WHITE MALLEE (Eucalyptus gracilis)

The species illustrated is the white mallee of western Victoria, known also as the red mallee in South Australia; it also occurs in western New South Wales and in Western Australia where it is known as 'snap and rattle'. Its common name is dependent on the colour of the inner bark and timber.

White mallee can be a mallee or a small tree from twenty to thirty feet high, with some rough bark at the base of the stems and smooth, grey or pale brown bark higher. It favours sandy soils, and flowers in winter or spring. It can be used as a windbreak species in semi-arid areas, as it is resistant to frost and drought. Other uses have been as firewood and for posts and props.

The name gracilis means 'slender', which is quite suitable, though this feature is not limited to this species.

PLATE 224

KANGAROO ISLAND GUM (Eucalyptus cneorifolia)

This species was originally described by Augustin de Candolle in 1828, from specimens collected on Kangaroo Island, in South Australia. It is mostly confined to the eastern end of that island, on limestone country, although it occasionally occurs on ironstone.

The name *E. cneorifolia* was given to this species to indicate the resemblance of its leaves to those of the European shrub, *Cneorum tricoccum*. Kangaroo Island gum can grow to fifteen or twenty feet, and occasionally as high as thirty feet, and it can be either a mallee or a small tree with mainly smooth bark, but some rough bark occurs on the stem. It flowers in late summer or autumn.

E. cneorifolia is frost-tolerant, moderately drought-resistant and tolerant of alkaline soils. It regenerates well after pruning or damage, and is a useful wind-break species. The species occurs at Encounter Bay in South Australia and at Kangaroo Island where it is the main species used in distilling eucalyptus oil on the island.

PLATE 225

SCALY BARK (*Eucalyptus squamosa*)

This is an uncommon species, occurring only in a limited area on sandstone ridges near Sydney, both to the south and to the north.

The common name and the botanical name both refer to the bark which is dark and scaly, somewhat resembling a bloodwood. *E. squamosa* is only a small tree reaching forty-five feet, with thick, lanceolate leaves and ovoid buds. The juvenile leaves are green and broadly lanceolate to almost circular in outline.

The position of this species in the classification of the eucalypts is doubtful. When it was originally described by Deane and Maiden in 1897 it was regarded as a distinct species but later Maiden named it as a variety of forest red gum (*E. tereticornis*). There appears to have been confusion between this species and calgaroo (*E. parramattensis* var. *parramattensis*), which it resembles in herbarium specimens, and which also grows mainly within one hundred miles of Sydney. The trees differ in bark type, juvenile leaves and anthers, and while *E. squamosa* occurs on dry ridges, *E. parramattensis* is found on heavy soils which are periodically waterlogged.

Flowering is possibly intermittent, but more in spring than at other times.

PLATE 226

RED MORREL (*Eucalyptus longicornis*)

Red morrel is one of the amazingly tall trees of a natural rainfall of from eleven to sixteen inches in the wheatbelt and goldfield area of southern Western Australia. It can grow up to seventy or eighty feet high, but is also seen as a smaller tree thirty to forty feet high. Rough bark covers the trunk for nearly half of the height, with smooth, grey or red-grey bark above. Mostly it grows in red or brown loam or sandy loam which is associated with calcareous subsoil.

Pointed buds, stalks usually longer than the fruiting capsule, shining leaves, and the typical bark and tree form mentioned above are reasonably good diagnostic features. The name *longicornis* means 'long-horned', a reference to the pointed buds. Another common name sometimes used is 'poot'. Flowers occur in summer.

Timber of the red morrel has been used in wheel-making and in mining work; the timber is strong and durable. Successful introductions of this species have been made in Cyprus and parts of Africa.

Individual trees of red morrel develop as a good park tree or shade tree. It is drought-resistant, frost-resistant and salt-tolerant.

PLATE 227

GIANT MALLEE (*Eucalyptus oleosa* var. *oleosa*)

A further species which is resistant to frost and drought, the giant mallee grows in the drier parts of southern mainland Australia. It is also known as red mallee and oil mallee. The name *oleosa* means 'oily', referring to the high amount of oil in the leaves; oil dots are copious. As the species is widespread, it is also variable, and a number of varieties have been recognised from time to time. However, the whole group of related species still needs clear delineation.

The giant mallee can be either a mallee or a tree up to about thirty feet high with rough bark stripping from the lower trunks and being smooth grey or light brown above this. It grows in sandy or loamy soil often associated with limestone.

The filaments are usually bent inwards, and the fruit, if fresh, has long, needle-like valves protruding. These valves are mostly broken off easily and thus may not be evident as a distinguishing feature. Flowering is in midsummer.

Slow-growing, with tough wood, the giant mallee can be used as a shade tree, windbreak, or for firewood or posts.

PLATE 228

(*Eucalyptus oleosa* var. *plenissima*)

An urn-shaped fruit and a short, rounded budcap are features of this dense mallee which can grow to about thirty feet. It has rough bark shedding in dark strips on the lower part of the stems, and above, the bark is smooth and grey. It grows mainly in sandy soil in a tract of country about sixty miles in diameter in the central wheatbelt of Western Australia, including near Dowerin and Mukinbudin.

This mallee is not common and has not earned itself a common name. The name *plenissima* means 'very full', a reference to the oil-rich, thick leaves. Very little cultivation of this mallee has taken place, and it may not provide anything better than a number of other species. As a windbreak or perhaps as low shade for stock, it could be useful. It is resistant to drought and frost, and flowers in midsummer.

PLATE 229

REDWOOD (*Eucalyptus transcontinentalis*)

Sometimes entirely with smooth, grey, or mottled, grey bark and sometimes having some dark grey bark shedding in strips near the base, redwood is either a tall mallee or a medium-sized tree from twenty to fifty feet high. Occasionally a specimen is taller. Redwood is also referred to as boongul and morrel, and botanically it has also been known as *E. oleosa* var. *glauca*.

This species is common in parts of the goldfields area of Western Australia in a large circle around Kalgoorlie, usually growing in sandy soil or gravelly loam. It has a spreading canopy and its creamy yellow flowers occur in spring. The leaves are grey or blue-green, often giving such a greyish appearance to the mallee that it is easily identified from afar. Abruptly pointed budcaps help further with identification.

If the seed source is known, attractive ornamental planting is possible, and the species is also suitable for windbreaks or as a shade tree, and for street planting. It is resistant to drought and frost, and its timber is tough and red, having been used for spear-making by the aborigines.

The name *transcontinentalis* refers to the fact that the species was thought to occur over much of southern Australia, but it is now recognised that this species is more restricted to Western Australia.

PLATE 230

CURLY MALLEE (*Eucalyptus gillii*)

Occurring on travertine limestone country on the Flinders Ranges, up to 400 miles north of Adelaide,

eastwards to Lake Frome, and in a few isolated areas near Broken Hill, *E. gillii* forms a silver cover over the hills. It is a mallee, growing in dense thickets, with smooth stems and sessile, heart-shaped or oval leaves which are arranged in pairs and are silver or blue-grey. The stems grow to about twenty feet tall and up to eight inches in diameter. The flowers are borne in umbels of about eight, in the axils of the leaves, the pale yellow flowers appearing in spring.

This species was named in honour of Walter Gill who was Conservator of Forests for South Australia and who sent the original specimens to J. H. Maiden in 1900.

E. gillii is closely related to the giant mallee (*E. oleosa* var. *oleosa*) and a variety with stalked leaves is now considered to be a hybrid between these two species.

The common name refers to the crooked growth of the stems.

PLATE 231

MERRIT (*Eucalyptus flocktoniae*)

Mostly this is a small tree about thirty to forty feet high, but sometimes it is a mallee. It has entirely smooth bark which is grey or brown, or sometimes mottled with these two colours; actually the older bark is grey as it sheds in patches, the new bark is pale brown. Red sandy loam in most of the lower rainfall area of southern Western Australia is the usual soil for merrit.

Merrit has attractive, alternate, shining, dark green, adult leaves, quite contrasting with the juvenile leaves which are opposite, grey, and decurrent on the stems. The tree is rapid-growing, and resistant to drought and frost; it is a good ornamental and street tree, and useful as a windbreak in drier areas. It flowers intermittently through the year but more in late winter to spring. The buds are often very distinctive by having a budcap of greater diameter at the base than the calyx.

Miss Margaret Flockton who was the main artist for J. H. Maiden's mammoth work *A Critical Revision of the Genus Eucalyptus* is honoured by the name of this species.

PLATE 232

DUNDAS MAHOGANY (*Eucalyptus brockwayi*)

This species was first collected in 1940 and described in literature the following year. It proved to be useful for tool handles during World War II, as its timber has a straight grain and long fibres. Only found in a small area around Norseman in Western Australia, the Dundas mahogany can grow as high as eighty feet, but is more usually between thirty and forty feet. It has smooth, grey to red-brown bark, and grows in brown to red sand or sandy loam.

E. brockwayi honours George Brockway who was formerly Superintendent of Inland Forests in Western Australia. The species has also been called Brockway's gum. It is vigorous and fast-growing, drought-resistant, and able to grow in rainfall of about ten inches annually; it is moderately resistant to frosts. As a shade tree, Dundas mahogany is excellent, with a spreading canopy, and its attractive bark and shining leaves make it a worthwhile ornamental tree. It is a good street tree in arid areas. Flowering time is from late summer to winter.

Globular, flask-shaped fruits are quite distinctive for the species, and an unusual feature is the foliage of seedlings which have small, narrow leaves. This stage changes when the plants are over a foot high.

PLATE 233

ROUND-LEAVED MALLEE (*Eucalyptus orbifolia*)

This is a rarely seen species which grows on and near some granite outcrops north of Southern Cross and west of Menzies in Western Australia. Despite being first collected in 1865, it has since been collected on comparatively few occasions from several limited localities. Consequently it is not very much cultivated, though it has much to recommend it as a small ornamental or possibly as a windbreak species. It is resistant to frost and drought, but may be slow-growing; one cultivated specimen was known to grow to about ten feet in ten years, reaching near maximum height as a small tree of twelve feet after twenty years.

In natural conditions, the round-leaved mallee usually grows to fifteen or twenty feet high, in granitic sands. Its bark is smooth and red-brown, always seen exfoliating in longitudinal strips; there is often a foot or two of rough, grey bark at the base. Glaucous stems, buds and fruits; stalked, rounded leaves, and a hemispherical fruit with sharply erect valves are useful features for aid in identification. It flowers mainly from April to August.

Both the common name and the specific name, *orbifolia*, refer to the rounded leaves which are unusual in *Eucalyptus*.

PLATE 234

SILVER MALLEE (*Eucalyptus crucis*)

The name *crucis* means a cross, referring to the town of Southern Cross, near which the species was first found. Sometimes the species is called Southern Cross silver mallee. It occurs in a few scattered localities with the centre between Kellerberrin and Kalgoorlie in Western Australia. As with some other comparatively rare species, it may later be found in new localities, for its known distribution at present represents collecting points accessible from good roads.

Similar to the round-leaved mallee (*E. orbifolia*), the silver mallee also grows in granitic sands in pockets on granite outcrops or round the base of such rocks. It is somewhat straggly in its natural habitat and tends to be similar in cultivation, being slow-growing, perhaps attaining five feet in eight or nine years. It could be improved, perhaps, by staking and light pruning to guide its growth. Growing to about twenty feet high, it has smooth, red bark which curls into longitudinal, tube-like strips as it exfoliates. It has heart-shaped, stalkless leaves, and glaucous stems, buds and fruits, the latter being convex or domed at the top.

Silver mallee flowers from November to January, and it is moderately frost-resistant and drought-resistant. A frost of fifteen degrees F in England has killed trees of the species, but it is growing satisfactorily in the Canberra Botanic Gardens.

PLATE 235

WEBSTER'S MALLEE (*Eucalyptus websterana*)

Smooth, red-brown bark which rolls longitudinally on the trunk when shedding is a marked feature of Webster's mallee. The species grows up to twenty feet in natural conditions, forming a dense, erect mallee or shrub with grey-green foliage; the obovate leaves usually have an indentation at the top, helping in identification.

The mallee has a very restricted distribution, being known mainly from near Coolgardie in Western Australia where it grows in red, granitic soil, and also from several areas in the MacDonnell Ranges of central Australia, but it is not abundant in any occurrence. C. A. Gardner, formerly the Government Botanist of Western Australia, has remarked on the fact that the curious bark of this species is also found on several other species which also occur on or around granite outcrops; such species are the silver mallee (*E. crucis*), gungurru (*E. caesia*) and the round-leaved mallee (*E. orbifolia*).

In cultivation this species will grow in sandy soils and maintain an erect, compact, but slightly spreading habit, with branches close to the ground. Fresh seed germinates readily. *E. websterana* can be recommended for growing in low rainfall areas, as its natural occurrence is in an area of about ten inches annually, but it will grow much better with more water. It flowers from March or April through to September.

PLATE 236
SALMON WHITE GUM (*Eucalyptus lane-poolei*)

While occasionally growing to fifty feet, salmon white gum is more usually seen as a tree from thirty to forty feet in height. It has a short trunk, often somewhat twisted, and the bark is smooth white to pinkish-yellow covered with a white or pale pink powder.

E. lane-poolei is named after Charles E. Lane Poole, a former Conservator of Forests in Western Australia. It is not a common tree; it grows in yellow, sandy gravel, in a small and narrow stretch of country from near Armadale, twenty miles south of Perth, southwards to near Waroona. Sometimes it may be confused with wandoo (*E. wandoo*) or powder bark wandoo (*E. accedens*), but it can always be separated from these by its rounded or egg-shaped buds and its more or less hemispherical fruits. The timber of salmon white gum is hard and straight, and red in colour, but is not used.

The species is suitable for use as an ornamental, preferably in a frost-free climate, but it can withstand light frosts and is moderately drought-resistant.

PLATE 237
EWART'S MALLEE (*Eucalyptus ewartiana*)

This mallee has a curious distribution, as it occurs in some red, sandy loams and gravelly sands in Western Australia in the wheatlands east and north-east of Perth and extending farther north-east into the less occupied areas. It also grows in mountain ranges in northern South Australia and in central Australia. The specific name compliments A. J. Ewart, a former professor of botany at the University of Melbourne.

Ewart's mallee has smooth, red bark which curls longitudinally as it sheds from the trunks, and it

mostly grows from ten to fifteen feet but can reach up to about twenty-five feet. Distinguishing features are green, oval-lanceolate leaves, a hemispherical or bluntly conic budcap and a more or less globular fruit. The species is resistant to drought and frost, and may be useful as a windbreak species. Its flowering time has not been recorded accurately, and actually may vary according to where the seed was obtained. W. F. Blakely recorded flowers in October and November.

PLATE 238
SHARP-CAPPED MALLEE (*Eucalyptus oxymitra*)

The common name, which is a translation of the specific name, is hardly distinctive, as many mallees have sharp caps, and in fact, this common name would hardly be in common usage, as the species is not common and grows only in areas which are sparsely settled. It grows in the northern part of South Australia and in adjoining areas of central Australia and Western Australia in deep, red sand, often in sand dune country, and in sands associated with mountain ranges. It is always a mallee, growing from twelve to fifteen feet, but occasionally to twenty-five feet high, with deciduous bark in strips low on the stems but smooth, grey or brown above.

The thick, oval-lanceolate, pale leaves and the almost globular fruits which are about half an inch in diameter are some features which aid in identification. Flowering time has not been recorded.

E. oxymitra does not appear to be in cultivation, no doubt because of its isolated occurrence, but it would be suitable for a windbreak species or as an ornamental shrub. It is drought-resistant and capable of resisting moderate frosts.

PLATE 239
TAMMIN MALLEE (*Eucalyptus leptopoda*)

The Tammin mallee is one of those species of which the common name is falsely indicative of a restricted occurrence, for this species occurs not only near Tammin, but over much of the wheatbelt and gold-field area of southern Western Australia. Commonly it is seen on roadsides, forming dense mallee thickets ten to twenty feet high in red or yellow-red sand. Slender stems sometimes have a few feet of rough bark near the base, but have smooth, grey to white bark above, becoming red-brown before shedding. Graceful, narrow foliage and the hemispherical to almost globular fruit are useful diagnostic features.

E. leptopoda is a further useful windbreak species, but could also be a good shrubbery plant. It is resistant to frost and drought, and flowers from December to March.

The name *leptopoda* means 'slender-stalked', referring to the slender pedicels and peduncles of the species.

PLATE 240

SALMON GUM (*Eucalyptus salmonophloia*)

The salmon gum has been regarded as an indicator of good, loamy soil on which much of the Western Australian wheatbelt is developed. Because of this, the species has been cleared from vast areas and forests are now mainly seen in the area east of Southern Cross. Trees of salmon gum up to eighty feet high are remarkable in an annual rainfall of eight inches, though it also occurs in areas with up to fifteen or twenty inches annually. Salmon gum is probably the main species which has been used as mining timber and in farm building and as firewood in the goldfield area of Western Australia. It is drought-resistant, moderately frost-resistant and slightly salt-tolerant, growing naturally in red sand or red-brown sandy loam. Flowers are seen from spring to summer.

The name *salmonophloia* means 'salmon bark', and the bark is indeed salmon-coloured and smooth, presenting a glorious sight in the arid areas in which it occurs. Small fruits, and buds like very small lemons, are additional characters helpful in recognition of salmon gum.

Salmon gum has been successfully cultivated overseas, and in a fifty inch rainfall in Kenya it has grown seven feet in just over a year. Its main use would seem to be for planting as timber, firewood, or ornament in arid zones, including street planting.

PLATE 241

GIMLET (*Eucalyptus salubris*)

The gimlet is often associated with salmon gum (*E. salmonophloia*) in rich, loamy soil, and this association once covered large tracts of country in the drier parts of southern Western Australia. Together these two eucalypts indicated the best farming land, and wheatfields now occupy most of this land. Gimlet forms pure stands in the more clayey soils and there are some good gimlet stands in the more arid goldfields area. It grows to forty or fifty feet in height, but is often less.

An outstanding feature is the trunk which is rich red-brown and smooth with flutings or spiralling quite prominent. This character, with shining, dark green leaves and obtuse, oval buds makes the gimlet easy to identify. The spiralling gave rise to the common name, but there have been other names which seem just as suitable. The early colonists called it the fluted gum tree and they also called it gimlet; sailors of the same period called it cable gum. The botanical name was a reference by Ferdinand von Mueller to what he termed the 'sanitary importance of the tree'.

Drought and frost-resistance and ability to grow in difficult clayey soils are attributes of this tree which is also of great beauty as an ornamental or as a street tree. It is highly successful as a street tree at Kalgoorlie in about a ten inch rainfall. Its timber is useful for poles, and the trees can be an attractive windbreak if planted in two rows. Flowers appear to be erratic, from March to October.

PLATE 242

FUCHSIA GUM (*Eucalyptus forrestiana*)

This is sometimes known as Forrest's marlock. It forms a mallee or a small tree from ten to fifteen feet high with smooth, grey or brown bark. The pendulous, four-winged buds with a long, narrow projection from the budcap makes the species unique. Only in a small area, mainly between Salmon Gums and Grasspatch in Western Australia, is the fuchsia gum found naturally, in gravelly, yellow loam. Flowers occur from midsummer to autumn, but the red buds are probably as attractive as the flowers and are present for a longer period.

Fuchsia gum is named after Sir John Forrest who was an explorer and also the first Premier of Western Australia. It has been cultivated in Australia and overseas, growing to nine feet in five years and achieving full height of about twelve feet in about ten years. Resistant to drought and frost, *E. forrestiana* is ideal as a hedge plant or as a garden shrub in either sandy or loamy soils, and in seaside areas.

PLATE 243

MOTTLECAH (*Eucalyptus macrocarpa*)

A sprawling shrub, mostly eight to ten feet high, but sometimes only about four feet, mottlecah is noticeable because of its silvery grey foliage. Its large, grey, conical budcap is most distinctive, and it has the largest fruit of any species of *Eucalyptus*, a feature noted by the botanical name which means 'large-fruited'. The bark is grey and smooth, and when the old bark sheds, the fresh stems are salmon-red.

The main distribution of this species is from Minginew to Piawanning, with some scattered occurrences eastward as far as Bruce Rock, in Western Australia. It is always in grey sand heath areas, and much of this country has been cleared in recent years.

In cultivation, mottlecah retains its sprawling form, but becomes more robust and its leaves are not then attacked by insects which cause frequent damage under natural conditions. The crimson flowers can occur at any time during the year, although the main flowering time is from winter to spring. Attractive specimens of mottlecah are features of the garden at Perth airport, Western Australia.

Mottlecah has also been called blue bush and desert mallee, and it is cultivated overseas as an ornamental. Though frost-tender when young, it is quite drought-resistant.

PLATE 244

ROSE MALLEE (*Eucalyptus rhodantha*)

A straggly, silver-leaved mallee which grows in grey-red sandy soil as a shrub up to eight feet tall, the rose mallee occurs about eight to ten miles south of Gunyidi siding in Western Australia. Although other localities have been mentioned in some references, no specimens exist to confirm these.

Typically, the rose mallee has distinctly stalked buds, and this feature separates it from the mottlecah (*E. macrocarpa*). The silver-grey leaves and the large, bright, red flowers make this species a most desirable garden ornamental. Flowers occur throughout the year.

The name *rhodantha* means 'rose-flowered', a reference to the normally crimson filaments, although the species occasionally has creamy filaments under natural conditions. It is resistant to drought, and may need protection from severe frosts.

PLATE 245

PEAR-FRUITED MALLEE (*Eucalyptus pyriformis*)

Always a mallee, this species grows to about eight to twelve feet high with smooth, grey-brown stems. Sometimes older shrubs become spreading and somewhat straggly. The species grows in red or yellow sand or sandy loam, and it can have creamy, yellow, or crimson flowers from June to October.

The pear-shaped buds are indicated by the name *pyriformis*, and these buds, together with the depressed, hemispherical fruits are indicative of the species. A sketch of the bud and fruit of this species is included in a panel of plant drawings on the current Australian five dollar note.

E. pyriformis occurs in the northern part of the wheatbelt of southern Western Australia and extends eastward into the arid areas north and north-east of Kalgoorlie. It is drought-resistant, and can withstand frosts to about twenty-five degrees F but may need protection when young. When pruned, the shrubs will coppice freely, and are highly suitable for hedges or windbreaks. The species is an excellent ornamental.

PLATE 246

LARGE-FRUITED MALLEE (*Eucalyptus youngiana*)

Very closely related to the pear-fruited mallee (*E. pyriformis*), but differing in having flowers without stalks, and fruits with strongly ridged, short-tubed calyces. The common name is misleading, for the species is often a small tree up to thirty feet high with rough bark covering about half of the height. It grows in red sand in the arid areas north and north-east of Kalgoorlie in Western Australia and extends eastwards into similar country in South Australia.

E. youngiana is drought-resistant and moderately frost-resistant and may be suitable for ornamental planting or for windbreaks in arid or semi-arid areas in sand or sandy loam. It flowers intermittently but mostly in spring and summer.

The botanical name honours a Mr Young who collected the specimen originally described.

PLATE 247

RED-BUD MALLEE (*Eucalyptus pachyphylla*)

Also known as the thick-leaved mallee, which is a translation of the name *pachyphylla*, this species grows in deep, red, sandy areas, including sand dunes, in central Australia and extending eastward, westward and southward just over the borders of the adjoining States. It is an extremely attractive mallee, with the red buds on short stalks and occurring in groups of three; the oval-lanceolate, grey-green leaves are thick and erect. Large, pale yellow or cream flowers are usually seen from May to September but predominantly in July to September. Red-bud mallee grows from six to fifteen feet high, with the bark peeling off in strips for about the lower three feet, then being smooth, grey-pink above.

Red-bud mallee is extremely drought-resistant and moderately frost-resistant and would make an excellent windbreak or hedge species in arid, sandy areas. It is a very attractive ornamental shrub, and the buds and fruits are most useful variations in dried or fresh floral arrangements.

PLATE 248

FINKE RIVER MALLEE (*Eucalyptus sessilis*)

A little known species, the Finke River mallee occurs only in ranges in central Australia, mainly the MacDonnell Ranges and some associated ranges. It is only found high on hillsides, particularly on sheltered slopes where it grows as a straggly mallee up to about twelve feet high, with dark grey bark peeling off in strips low on the stems and smooth, grey bark above. It is very closely related to the red-bud mallee (*E. pachyphylla*) and differs mainly in the buds and fruits being up to seven in a group and being without stalks. The name *sessilis* refers to the sessile, or stalkless, buds and fruits. Flowering is from May to September, and more in the later months of this period.

E. sessilis would be drought-resistant and moderately frost-resistant and could be used as an ornamental, hedge, or windbreak species. It was named Finke River mallee because of its occurrence in areas such as Palm Valley near the Finke River at Hermannsburg in central Australia.

PLATE 249

BURRACOPPIN MALLEE (*Eucalyptus burracoppinensis*)

This species differs from Oldfield's mallee (*E. old-fieldii*) by having stalks to its buds and fruits, and

striations or ridges on the budcap. In habit it is like Oldfield's mallee, being a dense mallee with branches close to the ground and spreading widely when not crowded for space. It grows mostly from twelve to fifteen feet high with some dark bark exfoliating at the base of the stems which are smooth and grey or grey-brown above. In the central part of Western Australia's wheatbelt, this mallee grows in red or yellow sands, and flowers from about September to January, particularly in November and December.

The habit of the Burracoppin mallee makes it an ideal windbreak species, and its large flowers are a recommendation as an ornamental. It is drought-resistant and moderately frost-resistant.

As with many other eucalypts, there would seem to be great scope for selection and breeding with this mallee to develop a highly suitable ornamental form.

PLATE 250

KINGSMILL'S MALLEE (*Eucalyptus kingsmillii*)

Named after W. Kingsmill, a former Member of the Legislative Council in Western Australia, this species grows in red sandy soil in the arid area of Western Australia, including Sandstone, Meekatharra, Lawlers and Carnegie. Its sculptured, ridged buds and fruits on stalks are different from its nearest relatives such as the red-bud mallee (*E. pachyphylla*), Finke River mallee (*E. sessilis*), pear-fruited mallee (*E. pyriformis*) and the large-fruited mallee (*E. youngiana*). There is some rough bark at the base of the stems, but the upper stems are smooth and grey. Mostly it is a mallee, but sometimes it is a small tree; it can be up to fifteen or twenty feet high but is more often about ten feet. Flowering time is in August and September.

Kingsmill's mallee is drought- and frost-resistant and could be an ideal ornamental shrub or windbreak species. In cultivation· in California it has attained nineteen feet in five years.

1 ILLYARRIE (*E. erythrocorys*)

2 TALLERACK (*E. tetragona*)

3 MALLALIE (*E. eudesmioides*)

4 SANDPLAIN MALLEE (*E. ebbanoensis*)

5 DARWIN STRINGYBARK (*E. tetrodonta*)

6 SCARLET GUM (*E. phoenicea*)

7 DARWIN WOOLLYBUTT (*E. miniata*)

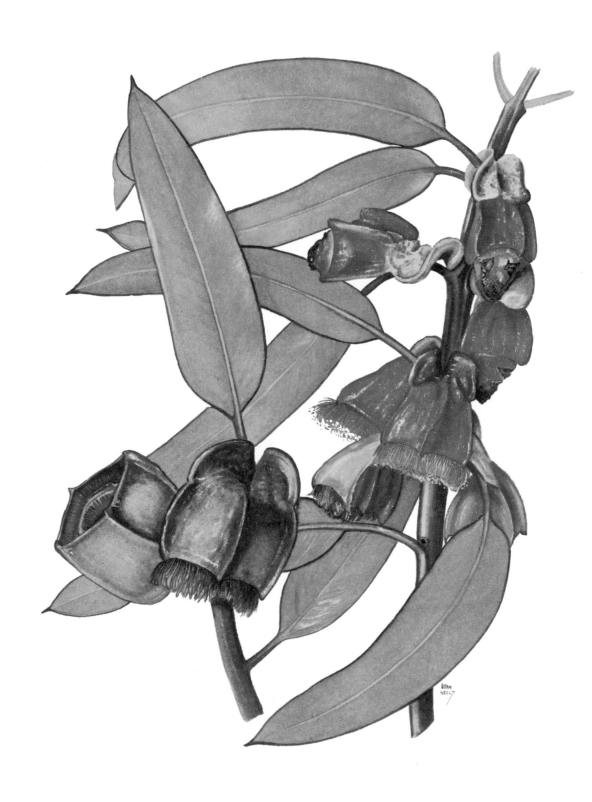

8 SQUARE-FRUITED MALLEE (*E. tetraptera*)

9 STEEDMAN'S GUM (*E. steedmanii*)

10 ROSEBUD GUM (*E. erythrandra*)

11 CARBEEN (*E. tessellaris*)

12 GHOST GUM (*E. papuana*)

13 ROUGH-LEAVED RANGE GUM (*E. aspera*)

14 ROUGH-LEAVED BLOODWOOD (*E. setosa*)

15 FAN-LEAVED BLOODWOOD (*E. foelscheana*)

16 SWAMP BLOODWOOD (*E. ptychocarpa*)

17   MARRI   (*E. calophylla*)

18 RED-FLOWERING GUM (*E. ficifolia*)

19 BROWN BLOODWOOD (*E. trachyphloia*)

20 BLOODWOOD (*E. terminalis*)

21 RED BLOODWOOD (*E. gummifera*)

22 YELLOW BLOODWOOD (*E. eximia*)

23 LEMON-SCENTED GUM (*E. citriodora*)

24 SPOTTED GUM (*E. maculata*)

25 KARRI (*E. diversicolor*)

26 ROSE GUM (*E. grandis*)

27   SYDNEY   BLUE   GUM   (*E. saligna*)

28 DEANE'S GUM (*E. deanei*)

29 BANGALAY (*E. botryoides*)

30 SWAMP MAHOGANY (*E. robusta*)

31 RED MAHOGANY (*E. resinifera*)

32 LARGE-FRUITED RED MAHOGANY (*E. pellita*)

33 SMALL-FRUITED GREY GUM (*E. propinqua*)

34 GREY GUM (*E. punctata*)

35 WOOLLYBUTT (*E. longifolia*)

36 CUP GUM (*E. cosmophylla*)

37 GUNGURRU (*E. caesia*)

38 LEMON-FLOWERED GUM (*E. woodwardii*)

39 SILVER-TOPPED GIMLET (*E. campaspe*)

40 STRICKLAND'S GUM (*E. stricklandii*)

41   GRIFFITH'S GREY GUM (*E. griffithsii*)

42 COARSE-LEAVED MALLEE (*E. grossa*)

43 YATE (*E. cornuta*)

44 WARTED YATE (*E. megacornuta*)

45 BUSHY YATE (*E. lehmannii*)

46 A FORM OF THE BUSHY YATE (*E. lehmannii* forma)

47 TUART (*E. gomphocephala*)

48 ROUND-LEAVED MOORT (*E. platypus*)

49 RED-FLOWERED MOORT (*E. nutans*)

50 OPEN-FRUITED MALLEE (*E. annulata*)

51 SWAMP MALLET (*E. spathulata* var. *spathulata*)

52 TALL SAND MALLEE (*E. eremophila*)

53 FLUTED HORN MALLEE (*E. stowardii*)

54 LONG-FLOWERED MARLOCK (*E. macrandra*)

55 FLAT-TOPPED YATE (*E. occidentalis*)

56 SALT RIVER MALLET (*E. sargentii*)

57 BLACK MARLOCK (*E. redunca* var. *redunca*)

58 BLACK-BARKED MARLOCK (*E. redunca* var. *melanophloia*)

59 BLUE MALLET (*E. gardneri*)

60 WANDOO (*E. wandoo*)

61   SUGAR GUM   (*E. cladocalyx*)

62 POWDER-BARK WANDOO (*E. accedens*)

63   DESMOND MALLEE (*E. desmondensis*)

64 YORK GUM (*E. loxophleba*)

65   COMET VALE MALLEE (*E. comitae-vallis*)

66 DUNDAS BLACKBUTT (*E. dundasii*)

67 LERP MALLEE (*E. incrassata*)

68   TWO-WINGED GIMLET (*E. diptera*)

69 PORT LINCOLN MALLEE (*E. conglobata*)

70 KANGAROO ISLAND MALLEE (*E. anceps*)

71 CONGOO MALLEE (*E. dumosa*)

72   GILJA   (*E. brachycalyx* var. *brachycalyx*)

73   CHINDOO MALLEE (*E. brachycalyx* var. *chindoo*)

74 CAPPED MALLEE (*E. pileata*)

75 KINGSCOTE MALLEE (*E. rugosa*)

76 ROUGH-FRUITED MALLEE (*E. corrugata*)

77 CLELAND'S BLACKBUTT (*E. clelandii*)

78 GOLDFIELDS BLACKBUTT (*E. lesouefii*)

79 JERDACATTUP MALLEE (*E. goniantha*)

80 CORAL GUM (*E. torquata*)

81 AUGUSTA WONDER (? *E. erythronema* var. *erythronema* × *E. torquata*)

82 TORWOOD (*E. torquata* × *E. woodwardii*)

83 RIDGE FRUITED MALLEE (*E. angulosa*)

84 SCARLET PEAR GUM (*E. stoatei*)

85 PIMPIN MALLEE (*E. pimpiniana*)

86 SPEARWOOD MALLEE (*E. doratoxylon*)

87 SLENDER MALLEE (*E. decurva*)

88 SILVER MALLET (*E. falcata*)

89 WHITE MALLEE (*E. erythronema* var. *erythronema*)

90 FLANGED WHITE MALLEE (*E. erythronema* var. *marginata*)

91 URRBRAE GEM (Hybrid with *E. erythronema* var. *erythronema* as the known parent)

92 CAP-FRUITED MALLEE (*E. dielsii*)

93 SHE BLOODWOOD (*E. exserta* var. *parvula*)

94 GREY MALLEE (*E. morrisii*)

95 FOREST RED GUM (*E. tereticornis*)

96 BLAKELY'S RED GUM (*E. blakelyi*)

97 TUMBLEDOWN GUM (*E. dealbata*)

98 DWYER'S MALLEE GUM (*E. dwyeri*)

99 CALGAROO (*E. parramattensis* var. *parramattensis*)

100 ROUND-BUDDED CALGAROO (*E. parramattensis* var. *sphaerocalyx*)

101 ORANGE GUM (*E. bancroftii*)

102 RIVER RED GUM (*E. camaldulensis*)

103 FLOODED GUM (*E. rudis*)

104 SNAPPY GUM (*E. brevifolia*)

105   WHITE GUM   (*E. alba*)

106 SWAMP GUM (*E. ovata*)

107 BROAD-LEAVED SALLY (*E. camphora*)

108 BLACK GUM (*E. aggregata*)

109 NARROW-LEAVED BLACK PEPPERMINT (*E. nicholii*)

110 WALLANGARRA WHITE GUM (*E. scoparia*)

111 BRITTLE GUM (*E. mannifera* ssp. *maculosa*)

112 APPLE-TOP BOX (*E. angophoroides*)

113 APPLE BOX (*E. bridgesiana*)

114 TENTERFIELD WOOLLYBUTT (*E. banksii*)

115 BUNDY (*E. goniocalyx*)

116 MEALY BUNDY (*E. nortonii*)

117   MANNA GUM   (*E. mannifera* ssp. *mannifera*)

118 CANDLE BARK (*E. rubida*)

119 MOUNTAIN GUM (*E. dalrympleana* ssp. *dalrympleana*)

120 TINGIRINGI GUM (*E. glaucescens*)

121 SPINNING GUM (*E. perriniana*)

122 BOOKLEAF MALLEE (*E. kruseana*)

123   *E. brachyphylla*

124 SILVER GUM (*E. crenulata*)

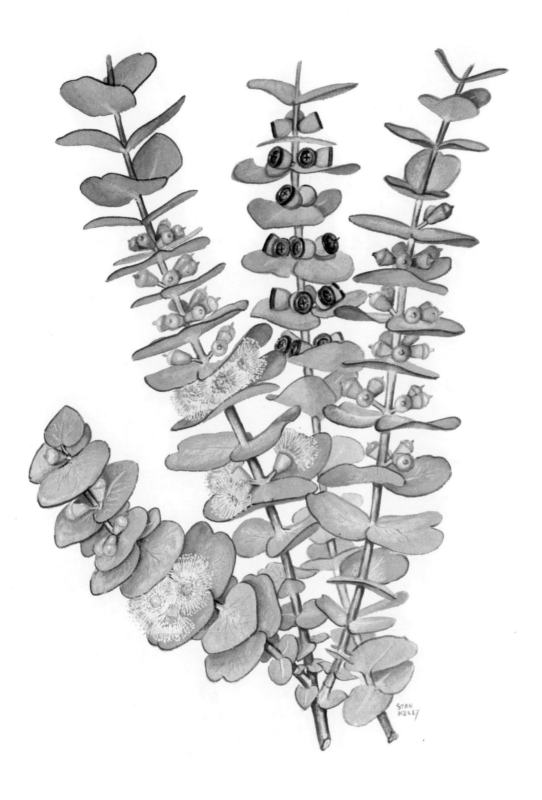

125   POWDERED GUM   (*E. pulverulenta*)

126 BELL-FRUITED MALLEE (*E. preissiana*)

127 BULLICH (*E. megacarpa*)

128 CROWNED MALLEE (*E. coronata*)

129 TASMANIAN BLUE GUM (*E. globulus*)

130 SOUTHERN BLUE GUM (*E. bicostata*)

131 MAIDEN'S GUM (*E. maidenii*)

132 MOUNTAIN GREY GUM (*E. cypellocarpa*)

133 BOG GUM OR FLAT-ROOT (*E. kitsoniana*)

134 OMEO GUM (*E. neglecta*)

135   YELLOW GUM (*E. johnstonii*)

136 CAMDEN WOOLLYBUTT (*E. macarthurii*)

137   GULLY GUM (*E. smithii*)

138 MANNA GUM (*E. viminalis*)

139 ROUGH-BARKED MANNA GUM (*E. huberana*)

140 ARGYLE APPLE (*E. cinerea*)

141   BLUE MALLEE (*E. gamophylla*)

142   GUM-BARKED   COOLIBAH   (*E. intertexta*)

143 GYMPIE MESSMATE (*E. cloeziana*)

144 SOAP MALLEE (*E. diversifolia*)

145 SWAN RIVER BLACKBUTT (*E. patens*)

146 WEEPING GUM (*E. sepulcralis*)

147 JARRAH (*E. marginata*)

148 YELLOW TINGLE (*E. guilfoylei*)

149   BLACKBUTT   (*E. pilularis*)

150 YELLOW STRINGYBARK (*E. muellerana*)

151 WHITE MAHOGANY (*E. umbra*)

152 TALLOW-WOOD (*E. microcorys*)

153 WHITE STRINGYBARK (*E. eugenioides*)

154 RED STRINGYBARK (*E. macrorhyncha*)

155 BROWN STRINGYBARK (*E. baxteri*)

156 GRAMPIANS GUM (*E. alpina*)

157 BLUE-LEAVED STRINGYBARK (*E. agglomerata*)

158 MESSMATE STRINGYBARK (*E. obliqua*)

159 BROWN BARREL (*E. fastigata*)

160 MOUNTAIN ASH (*E. regnans*)

161   ALPINE ASH (*E. delegatensis*)

162 SILVERTOP ASH (*E. sieberi*)

163 YERTCHUK (*E. consideniana*)

164 BASTARD TALLOW-WOOD (*E. planchoniana*)

165   YELLOW-TOPPED MALLEE ASH   (*E. luehmanniana*)

166 PORT JACKSON MALLEE (*E. obtusiflora*)

167 BLUE MOUNTAIN MALLEE ASH (*E. stricta*)

168 SNOW GUM (*E. pauciflora*)

169 BLACK SALLEE (*E. stellulata*)

170 LITTLE SALLY (*E. moorei*)

171 WHITE PEPPERMINT (*E. linearis*)

172 RIVER PEPPERMINT (*E. elata*)

173 ROBERTSON'S PEPPERMINT (*E. robertsonii*)

174 BLACK PEPPERMINT (*E. amygdalina*)

175 NARROW-LEAVED PEPPERMINT (*E. radiata*)

176 BROAD-LEAVED PEPPERMINT (*E. dives*)

177 TASMANIAN SNOW GUM (*E. coccifera*)

178 SILVER PEPPERMINT (*E. tenuiramis*)

179 NEW ENGLAND BLACKBUTT (*E. campanulata*)

180 SCRIBBLY GUM (*E. haemastoma*)

181 NARROW-LEAVED RED MALLEE (*E. foecunda*)

182 WHITE–LEAVED MALLEE (*E. albida*)

183 HOOK-LEAVED MALLEE (*E. uncinata*)

184 CRIMSON MALLEE BOX (*E. lansdowneana* var. *lansdowneana*)

185 WHITE-FLOWERED MALLEE (*E. lansdowneana* var. *leucantha*)

186 QUORN MALLEE (*E. porosa*)

187 PEPPERMINT BOX (*E. odorata* var. *odorata*)

188 SEASIDE MALLEE (*E. odorata* var. *angustifolia*)

189 BLUE MALLEE (*E. fruticetorum*)

190 GREEN MALLEE (*E. viridis*)

191 THOZET'S BOX (*E. thozetiana*)

192 NARROW-LEAVED BOX (*E. pilligaensis*)

193 BLACK BOX (*E. largiflorens*)

194 COAST GREY BOX (*E. bosistoana*)

195 BROAD-LEAVED MALLEE BOX (*E. behriana*)

196 NARROW-LEAVED GREY BOX (*E. woollsiana*)

197 INLAND GREY BOX (*E. microcarpa*)

198 GREY BOX (*E. moluccana*)

199 WHITE BOX (*E. albens*)

200 BIMBLE BOX (*E. populnea*)

201   COOLIBAH (*E. microtheca*)

202　NARROW-LEAVED RED IRONBARK (*E. crebra*)

203   LEMON-SCENTED IRONBARK (*E. staigerana*)

204   BLUE-LEAVED IRONBARK (*E. fibrosa* ssp. *nubila*)

205 BROAD-LEAVED RED IRONBARK (*E. fibrosa* ssp. *fibrosa*)

206 SILVER BOX (*E. pruinosa*)

207 SILVER-LEAVED IRONBARK (*E. melanophloia*)

208 GUM-TOPPED BOX (*E. orgadophila*)

209 GREY IRONBARK (*E. paniculata*)

210 CALEY'S IRONBARK (*E. caleyi*)

211   MUGGA   (*E. sideroxylon* ssp. *sideroxylon*)

212 YELLOW GUM (*E. leucoxylon* var. *leucoxylon*)

213 RED-FLOWERED YELLOW GUM (*E. leucoxylon* var. *macrocarpa*)

214 SCRUBBY BLUE GUM (*E. leucoxylon* var. *pauperita*)

215 YELLOW BOX (*E. melliodora*)

216 FUZZY BOX (*E. conica*)

217 SLATY GUM (*E. dawsonii*)

218 RED BOX (*E. polyanthemos*)

219 BLUE BOX (*E. bauerana*)

220 PINK GUM (*E. fasciculosa*)

221 GOOSEBERRY MALLEE (*E. calycogona* var. *calycogona*)

222 YEELANNA MALLEE (*E. calycogona* var. *staffordii*)

223 WHITE MALLEE (*E. gracilis*)

224 KANGAROO ISLAND GUM (*E. cneorifolia*)

225   SCALY BARK (*E. squamosa*)

226 RED MORREL (*E. longicornis*)

227 GIANT MALLEE (*E. oleosa* var. *oleosa*)

228   *E. oleosa* var. *plenissima*

229 REDWOOD (*E. transcontinentalis*)

230 CURLY MALLEE (*E. gillii*)

231 MERRIT (*E. flocktoniae*)

232 DUNDAS MAHOGANY (*E. brockwayi*)

233 ROUND-LEAVED MALLEE (*E. orbifolia*)

234 SILVER MALLEE (*E. crucis*)

235 WEBSTER'S MALLEE (*E. websterana*)

236 SALMON WHITE GUM (*E. lane-poolei*)

237 EWART'S MALLEE (*E. ewartiana*)

238 SHARP-CAPPED MALLEE (*E. oxymitra*)

239 TAMMIN MALLEE (*E. leptopoda*)

240 SALMON GUM (*E. salmonophloia*)

241 GIMLET (*E. salubris*)

242 FUCHSIA GUM (*E. forrestiana*)

243 MOTTLECAH (*E. macrocarpa*)

244 ROSE MALLEE (*E. rhodantha*)

245   PEAR-FRUITED MALLEE (*E. pyriformis*)

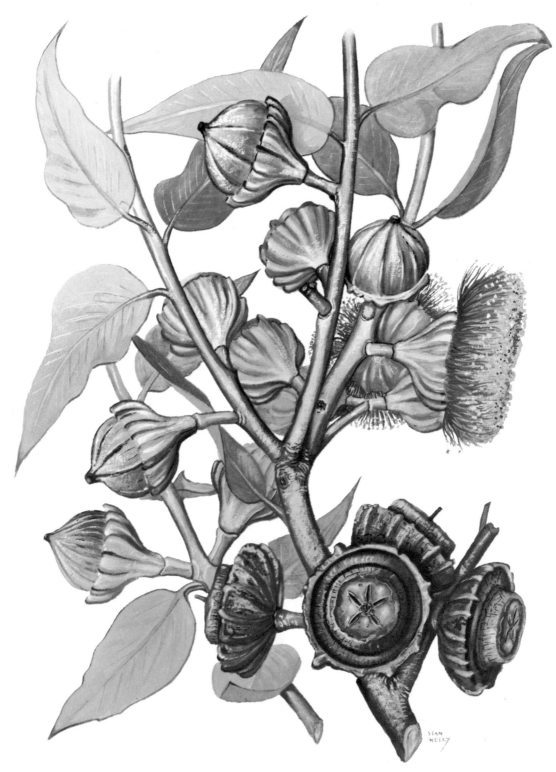

246 LARGE-FRUITED MALLEE (*E. youngiana*)

247 RED-BUD MALLEE (*E. pachyphylla*)

248 FINKE RIVER MALLEE (*E. sessilis*)

249 BURRACOPPIN MALLEE (*E. burracoppinensis*)

250 KINGSMILL'S MALLEE (*E. kingsmillii*)

Glossary

anther that part of a stamen which contains the pollen.

axil the angle between the stem and the leaf.

bloom a white covering formed by minute granules or platelets of wax. Also, a flower.

bole the main trunk of a tree.

calcareous containing calcium, usually as or from limestone.

calyx the outermost of the floral envelopes.

capsule a dry, many-seeded fruit, or 'gum-nut', which opens at maturity by slits or pores to shed the seed. In the case of eucalypts the capsule opens by valves.

corolla the inner floral envelope, often composed of separate petals, but united in the eucalypts, and sometimes joined to the calyx, to form an operculum.

crenulate having small, rounded teeth.

crown the branches and foliage of a tree.

cultivar a cultivated variety.

deciduous shedding the leaves annually. Certain eucalypts in northern Australia usually shed their leaves in unfavourable seasons and not necessarily annually.

disc the ring of tissue inside the staminal scar, on the top of a eucalypt capsule.

discontinuous distribution the condition when individuals occur in distinct areas separated by large areas without such individuals.

exfoliate to come away in flakes or scales, in this book usually referring to the bark.

exserted protruding beyond the mouth (of the capsule).

fibrous made up of woody fibres.

fruit the fertilised and developed ovary; in eucalypts it is generally taken to include the floral tube in which the ovary is embedded, and is woody, not succulent.

genus the smallest natural group containing distinct species; the name of the genus forms the first part of the name of the species.

glaucous originally sea-green, but in botany now meant to convey an ashy or grey-green appearance, like a cabbage leaf.

habit form or manner of growth.

habitat the kind of locality in which a plant grows.

herbarium a collection of dried plants, used for reference and as a basis for studies of relationships.

igneous as in igneous rocks, which are rocks formed in a fluid condition beneath the surface of the earth and are sometimes extruded, as from a volcano, or else solidified beneath the earth. References in this book are to soils derived from igneous rocks.

lanceolate narrow, tapering to each end; in modern use, with the greatest breadth at about one-third from the base.

lateritic referring to a soil with an accumulation of iron concretions, usually as a result of a fluctuating water table.

lignotuber a swollen woody mass at the base of the stem and usually just below the soil surface, containing numerous dormant buds.

linear narrow, several times longer than wide, with parallel sides.

mallee a eucalypt with several stems arising from a lignotuber.

mat with a fine-textured, dull, surface.

mealy like meal, powdery, dry, soft.

operculum the budcap, or lid of the eucalypt flower-bud, formed by fusion of the petals; an outer operculum may be formed by the calyx, or both calyx and corolla may be united.

orbicular disc-shaped, a flat body with a circular outline.

ovate shaped like a longitudinal section of a hen's egg.

ovoid an egg-shaped solid.

panicle a compound inflorescence; in eucalypts, composed of a series of umbels arranged on a branched common stalk.

pedicel the stalk of a single flower.

peduncle the common stalk of a group of flowers.

petals the individual organs which form the corolla.

petiole the stalk of a leaf.

75

pollination the placing of pollen on the stigma of a flower.

reversionary having the form of an earlier stage of development.

sapling a young tree.

savannah grassland characterised by scattered trees, especially in tropical and sub-tropical regions.

scion a cutting, shoot or twig selected for grafting on to other stock.

scrub vegetation dominated by low woody plants.

sepals the individual organs which form the calyx.

sessile without a stalk.

spathulate oblong, narrowed towards the base.

species the basic unit in classification; a population or system of populations of individuals which normally interbreed.

specific name the generic name plus a specific epithet.

stamen a male organ of a flower, consisting of a filament bearing an anther which contains pollen.

striated marked with fine lines, or grooves.

tessellated divided into small, approximately square units, like tiles.

topography the shape and locality of natural features on the earth's surface; originally the description or mapping of such features.

tubercle a wart-like knob.

twig a small branch; usually the smallest branches of a tree.

understorey the lower layer of vegetation; plants growing in the shelter of the uppermost, exposed layer.

umbel an inflorescence composed of a cluster of flowers whose pedicels arise from the same point.

valves the teeth-like units into which the top of a capsule separates at maturity.

vegetative propagation the production of new plants without using seeds. This is usually done by using cuttings, which produce their own roots, or grafting a scion on to an already rooted stock.

venation collective vein pattern on leaves.

Index

Page numbers in italics refer to Plates; numbers in bold type indicate major entries.